SEX FUN

By Anthony Harris and published by New English Library

WATER EXERCISES
YOUR SKIN
SEX FUN

SEX FUN

A Joygivers' Manual

Anthony Harris Ph.D M.Sc

NEW ENGLISH LIBRARY

A New English Library Original Publication, 1983

First NEL Paperback Edition November 1983

NEL Books are published by
New English Library,
Mill Road, Dunton Green,
Sevenoaks, Kent.
Editorial office: 47 Bedford Square, London WC1B 3DP

Typeset by Fleet Graphics, Enfield, Middlesex

Made and printed in Great Britain by
Hunt Barnard Printing Ltd., Aylesbury, Bucks.

British Library C.I.P.

Harris, Anthony, 1937–
Sex fun.
I. Title
612'.6 HQ31

ISBN 0–450–05374–1

CONTENTS

Bondage • Slaps and Corporal punishment • Humiliation • Arab straps, love-balls and enlargers • Clitoral and vaginal stimulators • Performance creams and pills • Sex books and magazines • Vibrators • Dildoes

RESOURCES

Personality • Sexual approach • Physique • Gentleness • Menstruation • Semen • Contraception — Sheaths: Diaphragms and caps: The Pill: Coils: Pessaries: Holding back and withdrawal: First aid: Sterilisation: Rhythm method • Proception • Pregnancy • Fidelity • Infidelity • Fats • Energy • Crying • Barter • Memory aids — Photography: Tapes: Video

INTRODUCTION

THIS BOOK is dedicated to couples of long standing, closely bound by shared interests and real affection. Sometimes such people find themselves overfamiliar with their spouses, comfortably accepting the ennui that other couples seem to escape.

We found that couples with the most relish for sex did not wait for it to present itself: they presented themselves to sex. Just as you have breakfast in the morning (or should), go through the rituals of dinner, and of your everyday life, so they, with the same amount of effort and forethought, went about sex. This attitude works well.

You take mishaps in your working life in your stride, so when sex is ordinary, it certainly is no cause for sulks or bad temper – or divorce. When sex is really good, however, you anticipate it more the next time round. An open attitude will help you escape familiarity and boredom, and you can learn about the many things to do to keep sex pleasurable.

In compiling this book I was guided by two main principles. First, the only people who really know about sex fun are those who enjoy sex thoroughly. Secondly, sexuality is as varied as the people who express it. Accordingly, I gathered experiences from people whose enjoyment of sex was as obvious as the shining sun.

Regarding the organisation of the book. Fun can be hearty or jovial, with grins or laughs, giggles or chuckles. Sex, too, has many faces. Accordingly, I have gathered methods and techniques together and set them in sections such as Smiles, Chuckles, Laughs. Obviously this is a flexible convention, as it should be, since what may be a titter for you, may be a belly laugh for someone else. Even with your own partner, a section in Smiles may lead you to robust sexuality, and another in Laughs may merely titillate while he or she reacts the opposite way. Nevertheless, fun has been emphasised for both. We are, after all, the only creatures to laugh and to make love all year round. May these two unique features gladden you both.

SMILES

Smiling

LOOK INTO a mirror, face on. Close your eyes. Think of the happiest time of your life. Picture it. Feel your muscles working. The smile is coming, so let it come. Now open your eyes, and give your smile a little help. Let the lips part. Crinkle your eyes. Curl the edges of your mouth up. Nine people out of ten now laugh. Did you? If not, try again.

The strange thing is that when you smile fully, even when practising like this, you'll feel better. This is because the nerves that lead from your brain to your smile muscles are activated by feelings of happiness. So when you make the muscles work in the right way, the message goes back to your brain: 'I am happy'.

A real smile involves special muscles. All other movements of the face, though they may look like smiles, aren't true ones. You have muscles around your mouth, under the lips, over the lips, but the smile muscle starts at the edge of the mouth and goes up to the cheek-bone. It has the jaw breaking name of *zygomatic major*. When you really smile, this is the muscle that goes into action. It can be the prelude to other muscles working well.

A real smile pulls the lips up into a curve, with each side balanced. It is genuine when the pull is so strong that the lips part and the eyes crinkle.

So powerful is the smile from the heart that if you smile genuinely at your partner, you'll get a quick response.

Blushing

BLUSHING IS caused by a sudden surge of blood to the skin, giving a warm tingling feeling. In sexual excitation your blood vessels expand due to the release of hormones. Too much *epinephrine*, or adrenalin, released from your kidneys results in tenseness and a pale skin. But when the amount is right, blushing occurs.

Among the chemical cupids responsible for these changes are the *endorphins*, pleasure chemicals which are produced naturally in the body and help relax you. Sexual excitement is caused by a mixture of hormones being produced, and laboratory findings have shown that healthy people flush more readily than depressed ones. In a survey of more than 350 women, those experiencing sexual satisfaction reported that blushing in their partners was associated with a high degree of potency, and they themselves found that their sexual expression was better when they felt skin flushes whether on the face or other parts of the body. Certainly when blushing occurs, the skin also gets hotter.

For couples of long standing, the blush can be used as a silent indicator of what promises well for sexual fun. So, as you try out various new ideas in this book, watch out for the blush. If it comes, you know you have discovered another source for sexual pleasure in whatever caused it.

Some people blush more easily on different parts of their bodies, so I have graded them for sex-fun promise: the higher the score the more fun you've had or are going to have.

Blush on the ear-lobes A good sign: your partner still has the ability to respond easily to sex, but likes to hide it to some extent. Score 5.

Blush on the cheeks An even better sign, especially if the partner is also smiling, because clearly his or her sexual interest in you is strong and uninhibited. Score 5.

Blush on the throat Your partner is serious about sex with you. Score 10.

Body blush The greater the extent, the greater the arousal and the greater the expectation of fun. Score 20.

The non-blusher If nothing you can say, do or show can raise a blush, then the chances are you have a non-starter. Score zero.

You sometimes have to look very carefully for the tell-tale sign, because research is incomplete. Indeed, you may discover a new blush zone – the feet perhaps?

Breasts

THE BREASTS lure the sex partner more dramatically than the rest of the body – their shape is obvious anywhere, at any time. Women have the largest breasts of any warm-blooded animal for their body size, larger than the requirement for producing milk warrants.

Many babies are breast-fed. The breast is a warm, soothing place, which the infant learns to associate with comfort and satisfaction. This association is carried over to adult life. Even bottle-fed babies are fondled and cradled by their mothers at the breast, so the effect is felt by them too. This learned, favourable response to breasts is just as strong in women as in men, and is one of the reasons why women like looking at other women.

The most easily aroused part of the breasts is the nipple.

Stroking, licking, sucking and very gentle biting cause them to pop out; sometimes they become three to four times normal size. Just as you can't tell how large a penis is when it is relaxed, so you can't tell how large the nipples are until blood rushes into and erects them. Because of its stippled surface, the nipple can give and take pleasure from tongue, penis and another nipple. Male nipples, of course, are included in this. For this reason, neither partner's nipples should ever be ignored in love-making.

During sexual play, the breasts and nipples swell as blood flows into them. The aureole, the coloured part around the nipple, is sensitive to tickling with the finger tips and the penis head. Sometimes great care and patience is required to make the blood flow, but in some women the flow comes with such force that it can be felt pumping into the vesicles – spaces in the breast to receive the blood. Often the breast blushes – a sure sign of sexual sincerity – but again it is not easy to produce this reaction. Get your partner to tell you how.

The swelling can be so great as to increase the breasts by a cup size, but once orgasm is reached, they subside. Obviously, if you don't give your lover orgasm after her breasts have swollen in sexual anticipation, she's going to be frustrated and, rightly, will feel cheated. If this happens too often, her breasts won't respond warmly – like an inexperienced girl's. In time, rather than face disappointment, women with bad lovers turn off.

A majority of women, particularly as they get older, do not get sexually excited through the breasts. In itself this is not a bad thing, but it is rather like settling for half a loaf. Non-arousal of the breasts can occur in a woman when her partner is potent, able to sustain an erection with hard thrusting for at least 15 minutes. The woman knows she can achieve orgasm, and neither partner pays much attention to her breasts in what is usually a short period of foreplay. In this robust situation, both would have even more memorable and satisfying climaxes if they did not ignore the nipples and breasts during intercourse.

Breast tissue extends into the armpit. Stroking up from the waist, over the hollow of the armpit, then onto the arm and back along, then over the chest and round the breast itself, is very soothing and relaxing. Do it lightly and it tickles. In a long-term relationship, husbanding like this is essential.

Once the breast is healthily stimulated it can take the pressure of a full embrace, chest to bosom, and squeezing, and the sliding of the shaft of the penis between the cleavage – but only at this stage.

During menstruation breasts increase in size and are often extremely tender, so that even gentle caressing can be painful. But many women like to have intercourse during menstruation, so a little consideration is needed to avoid misunderstanding. She's keen one moment, and then in the next complains that his ardour is hurting her – and it may well be. Go gently. After the period, the breasts usually revert to their robust selves.

One of my subjects charted her sexual responses during pregnancy. As her breasts grew larger, swollen, the skin tight and heavily veined, she wanted her husband to pay more and more attention to them. When she had her child, she breast-fed. She reported deep satisfaction from this, a feeling warm and sexual in nature.

This last finding explains a lot. To ensure reproduction of our species, sex is exciting and full of good feelings. However, women who put sex in one category – their vaginas – are often alarmed at the sensuousness of breast-feeding, although the feeling is merely Nature's way of making pleasurable an often tiring aspect of baby-care. To be accurate, the feeling is not essentially sexual: it is joy in living.

Body language

WISE LOVERS can use body language to enrich their lives, because they have through their experiences with one another a whole theatre of memories, ready to be staged again on the right cue – and that cue will be one of the old and tried, barely consciously noticed body hints.

When people love each other they copy each other's body positions, in bed, at restaurant tables, on park benches and on the beach. So strong is the link that even if you wanted to hide your feelings from the other person, you automatically give yourself away by echoing everything they do. Consequently, you can pick out lovers, even when they are trying to hide it, just by seeing how closely they fall into step, do a sort of long drawn out dance by copying each other's movements even when talking about the weather or the job in hand.

But body language can tell you a lot about yourself too. When you are depressed, your shoulders automatically sag, and your back becomes rigid instead of being flexible. When you are tense, it is not only your emotions that are being bottled up. Your tummy muscles tighten and your walk becomes jerky.

The reason is that anxiety and tension affect the messages coming from your brain to your body – unconsciously. Instead of muscles contracting only when they should – when doing their work, for example – they get messages to tighten up even when they should be resting. So being tense means exactly what it says.

This affects the way you stand: usually the legs are kept too close together, the arms stiff at the sides. Look around you, in the street, in shops, at work. Notice how some people have loose, relaxed postures, while others are rigid.

People who are open and unembarrassed will talk to you with movements of their arms, facing you. The inhibited or shy, or people who do not know you at all, tend to avert their faces. They also tend to cross their arms, or at least hold them in front, as if they were a kind of shield.

Such body language is the real test of what is going on inside you, and between you and other people. No matter what you may actually say, the real message is there in what your body does. Check the signs on this scoring guide.

Body Language Scores

When at meals Put your elbows on the table. If your partner follows suit, score 1. If they do something entirely opposite, for example, leaning back or folding their arms, score zero.

On the settee If your arm is over the back of the settee and your legs are crossed, the intimate partner will be facing you with arm over the settee and legs crossed. Copying, score 1; entirely different, score zero.

When talking while standing up Put all your weight on one

leg. If they follow suit, score 1; if they stand firmly on two feet, score zero.

In a group on the beach If the person you are interested in is copying your position, score 1; if they are copying someone else's, score zero.

When walking Change step. If your companion makes an effort to get back into step, score 1; otherwise, zero.

Add up the scores. A total of 3 or above indicates that an enviable state of intimacy reigns. Less than 3? Perhaps it's time to concentrate on one another a little more.

Eyes

WHEN YOU dislike something or someone, the pupils of your eyes narrow to pinholes as you look at the object. People unconsciously note this, and they may react with the stony glare too. Result? Even before a word is uttered, you will both be on the defensive.

As intimacy progresses between two people, they take each other's faces in as they chat. The eyes meet, just long enough to register, and then move to the mouth, the cheeks, the hair. A man interested in a woman actually traces her figure out with his eye movements. Of course, women do the same with men. Trace each other out – and watch the pupils grow.

As a poet once quipped: 'Candy is dandy, but liquor is quicker'. What he didn't know was that the pupils of the eyes actually widen to three or four times their size when you've been drinking. This gives a soft and misty look. Smoking actually causes the pupils to shrink.

Blinks

USUALLY WE blink about twice a second. The more relaxed you are, the slower the blink; but when you are sexually interested in someone, your blink rate goes up, and there is nothing you can do about it.

To get some idea of how much the pupil varies, sit in front of a mirror with a light shining into your eyes. Cover up your eyes with your hands and shut them. After a few minutes open them, looking into the mirror. You'll just catch the pupil large, and then it gets smaller as the light begins to affect it.

Eyes smouldering with passion refers to this physiological fact. It happens because pleasure releases relaxing hormones which affect the nervous control of the eye, relaxing the little muscles in the coloured part, the iris, so the pupil gets bigger.

The reverse happens when suspicion or dislike is present. Then the chemistry of your bloodstream tells you to beware and the whole body tenses, including the pupil control muscles, so the pupil gets beady.

When you first meet today glance at the eyes. Bright eyes, with a sunny-sky-tinge to the white, invariably means alertness. A good start. If he or she looks into your eyes, and there's an opening of the pupil, there is interest, even if the manner may not show it.

Watch the blink rate. If it goes up, move in. Otherwise you may have wasted an opportunity.

Ear-lobes

EXTRAORDINARY EFFECTS can be obtained by sucking, tweaking, stroking, and kissing these boneless wonders. Don't neglect the area underneath them, since many people find that even more stimulating.

Feet

THERE ARE many erotic spots in the feet, about the ankle and on the sole, which respond to pressure. The exact mechanism is not understood, but broadly speaking the stimulation of these areas release relaxant hormones from the nervous system – a group of endorphins – which certainly help sexual play.

Dressing the foot up in various shoes turns some people on, so it is well worth experimenting with galoshes, high heels, and silk slippers.

Kissing and cuddling

THESE AFFECTIONATE acts tend to be neglected as time goes by in a relationship. A pity, and a mistake, since they create an unbeatable foundation for sexual warmth, and are marvellous starters for sex fun.

You kiss each other's nipples, armpits, knees, buttocks, genitalia, eyes, mouth. You kiss with lips closed, with lips open, with tongue out, with tongue in. You smile, talk, laugh, blow, suck and hum as you are kissing. Humming sets up vibrations that are effective on belly, vulva, glans, earlobes and forehead.

We British are too distant, even from our loved ones. Children brought up in kiss-and-cuddle homes are happier. They even develop quicker mentally and physically. In adult life, love can go out of the window when joy does, so check out your kiss-and-cuddle rating. Score 1 for yes, zero for no.

When waking up Do you kiss your lover?
When saying goodbye Do you kiss him or her?
When meeting after work Do you kiss?
When watching TV Do you cuddle up, even if only during the commercials?
Hugging Did you hug your partner today?
Holding hands Do you ever hold hands?
When talking Do you put your arms around his or her neck when talking?
Saying good night Do you kiss good night?
Sleeping Do you fall asleep in each other's arms? Or cuddled up?
Wakening Do you awaken in each other's arms? Or cuddled up?

Rating

If your total score is 7 or more: no one needs to tell you how happy you are! If it is 4 to 6: since you have a little of a good thing, why not try for more? Less than 4: chill winds are blowing: perhaps you had better kiss and cuddle to get a rosy glow against the frost of no-fun sex.

Your skin is more than a protective covering. It has invisible kiss spots and cuddle lines where touch can work miracles of good feeling.

This means that kissing can help your aches and pains, because not only are the lips warm, but a good smacking kiss also exerts a lot of pressure, like a massage. Moreover, salivary glands produce fluids which heal cuts and abrasions, so the moisture on your lips has special properties.

The kissing starter for sex fun goes like this:

A smacker on the forehead, keeping in contact for a count of ten.

Three little kisses on the neck, one on the nape, one each on both sides.

A long kiss to the count of five on the front of each ankle. (Now you know why Elizabethan courtiers did this.)

Smackers for the count of seven at the back of each knee. This really tickles, so be careful you don't kick each other.

Three long kisses, to the count of ten each, one inch exactly below the belly button.

Finally, a gentle long kiss on the lips.

Cuddling not only gives big-area warmth, but also big contact. The cuddle starter for sex fun goes like this:

Arms around the waist, hug for the count of three, and the same again another two times.

Hug around the shoulders, a real bear hug, three times to the count of five.

Hug around the hips, kneeling for this; bear hug three times to the count of four.

You can put the kiss-and-cuddle sex fun starters together and have yourself kissed and cuddled to bliss. The kisser and cuddler also gets a lot out of it, because the pressure of the hugs and kisses are relaxing as well as exciting.

Next time you feel blue, with frets and headaches, don't reach out for a pill, kiss and cuddle your lover. You can start off cold. The rest will follow.

Research shows that headaches come from tension in the neck muscles, shoulders and the very thin, easily stressed muscles on the forehead. When you get uptight and frown, your muscles knot up. Relaxation is all you need, but how to get it? That's where the kissing and cuddling comes in.

Heat is a great relaxer, one of the reasons why lying in the sun is so popular, and everyone knows what a warm bath or shower can do for you. But the body produces enough heat every 30 minutes to boil a small kettle. This heat passes through your lips quickly because the skin there is so thin, and the circulation there is so near the surface – that's why your lips are red. All of your body gives off heat, so kissing and cuddling is a great relaxer, especially when you kiss or get kissed on those parts of the body which are specially sensitive.

The bonus is that as the headaches, frets, and irritations fade away, better feelings take their place, and the kiss-and-cuddle cure becomes the best cure of all: love.

Navel

BE GENTLE with it, because it can be easily damaged. Use the navel mainly as a superb compass point. Two-and-a-half centimetres up, and you'll find a particularly sensitive place to massage and kiss. Two-and-a-half centimetres down, it's the same, and even better five centimetres down.

Penis

EVEN COUPLES with good sex lives have crossed wires of communication with regard to the sensitivity of this organ and its associated scrotum.

Some things he may not have told you

The tip and head of the penis is too sensitive for fingers to be rubbed on it. It feels like sandpaper would on the clitoris. If you pull the foreskin back too hard, it is like being skinned alive. In the case of circumcised men, pulling down on the shaft skin is also like being skinned alive.

The testicles are extremely delicate. Even moderate pressure causes pain. However, warm grasping, lifting, twirling, stroking with fingertips, all are very pleasurable indeed. Teeth hurt the penis. During oral sex make sure the tongue covers the bottom teeth, and your upper lip is curled over the upper ones.

If you squeeze too tightly with your vaginal muscles as he enters, you can bruise him.

Some things she may not have told you

Your penis is something too big to be thrust into her mouth. She does not like to gag on it. If you do push it in, do it gently, and use teasing techniques. Oral sex for many women is a literal pain in the neck, because some men grab them around the head and push them down. Dominance can be good sex fun, but if you get your cues mixed up, and your partner doesn't want domination, you'll spoil it.

Many women like to play with the penis and testicles. They will appreciate your lying still to let them have their way. Women resent your intrusion when they are with *their* penis.

The natural secretions of a clean penis are thoroughly arousing, but an unwashed one is a turn off. All you need to do is wash the head and behind the skin in the morning and at night. You don't need any extras, though perfume on the scrotal hairs is a nice surprise, as long as the more tangy, unmistakable pheronomes of the penis head are left intact.

Vulva and vagina

VAGINA AND vulva are not synonymous. The vulva comprises the lips, the hairs, the mons, the minor lips, the clitoris, the urethral opening and the opening of the vaginal passage. The vagina is the canal behind the vulva up to the cervix at the top.

What he may not have told you

He finds your natural smells and juices arousing, but can live without getting a mouthful of aluminium oxide during oral sex. Deodorants for the vulva and vagina are unnecessary.

Many women appear not to realise that their thigh muscles are very strong, easily capable of breaking a man's jaw when he is kissing the vulva. Gentle thigh control is a must.

What she may not have told you

Please check that your fingernails are short and smooth before vaginal massage. Please remove rings that may cut vaginal skin. Be gentle when going over the urethral opening (tucked under the clitoris, which covers it like a flap, except when it is erect). It gets sore very easily.

Nibbling the vulva requires a finesse if it isn't to be traumatic. Practise with a grape. Roll it around your tongue and try to hold it between your teeth without rupturing it.

Hair

HUMAN HAIR is unusual in its nature, distribution, colouring and sexual function, and has few parallels in the animal kingdom.

Prior to sexual maturity we have hair on our heads, eyelids and eyebrows, but nowhere else, although there is tiny, very thin, functionless hair all over the body. There appear to be three basic pigments in hair: red, blue, and yellow. Mixed they give black: if red and blue are missing, it gives blond.

Hair itself is a protein, similar to that of the nails. It has a scaly surface and a central core in which the pigment is contained. It grows from modified sweat glands, which also produce oily secretions. This leads to different odours, red-heads in particular seeming to produce a very individualistic aroma. Even though both sexes grow hair at the pubis, it is like an upside down triangle in females and like an upright triangle in males. Why this difference exists is an unsolved mystery, but see later.

As people get older, the hair coarsens and eventually turns grey because pigment is no longer manufactured. Women seldom lose their head hair, while men begin to lose theirs as early as the middle twenties. The one sure cure for baldness in men is to take female hormones, (present in women's urine and vaginal juices). It then sprouts very well, but at the same time, hips can get curvy and breasts may grow. So flaunt your baldness!

The glands of the armpit and near the genitals produce very strong scents, differing from person to person, but they are automatically sexually exciting. The hair here actually acts as a sponge, retaining scent. Even if you insist that armpit odours offend you, your sexual trigger is still pulled.

During intercourse, pubic hair acts as a dry lubricant, but this practical function pales before the dramatic psychological effects. The plum-red penis head rising from a forest of black, blond or brown hair is that much more obvious against its contrasting background. Similarly, the pink lips of the open vagina, hedged by hair, are emphasised and put in frame. You see the picture immediately. Try the cameo.

Letting your hair down means releasing inhibitions. In highly civilised communities, women go in for elaborate and refined hair styles, enhancing the natural beauty of the hair itself and revealing the face or hiding it, revealing the neck or accentuating it. She is on show publicly – but in the bedroom, the pins and combs come out, and the hair cascades down. She is released from being on show and is ready to let herself go. This hair display excites the partner too.

Another variant of hair display is putting both hands on the neck and raising the hair to reveal the neck. (In Japan this was once considered extremely provocative, equivalent to striptease.) If nude, this action also shows the armpit hair, which contrasts so strikingly with the breasts. Hair shows are recommended.

Male hair display has taken different forms. In Prussian society they shaved their heads, taking to extremes what nature had already done for some in proclaiming masculinity by giving them a bald pate. Modern skinheads also take this as a sign of violent masculinity. Long hair in a man, unless he is very young or a hippy, is even today regarded as the province of mad professors (where it is simply neglect) and musicians (where it is traditional). It is revealing that long-haired pop stars have hairless chests, like the young Mick Jagger. They appealed not to women, but to teenie boppers, whose own sexuality is not ready for the sweaty, hairy chest of the balding man. These idols are girlish, giving their teenage female fans more scope for fantasising sex instead of facing up to real sexuality. However, other pop stars, like Gary Glitter, have capitalised on a butch, daddy-figure image: chest hair, belly, and all. Adam Ant is at least muscular.

I have surveyed several hundred women on baldness and sexual attractiveness. For some extraordinary reason, young girls seem to hate baldies. Most women reported that they hardly noticed, performance potential being far more important. Some women reported that seeing a bald pate between their legs or on their chests was a turn-on.

A beard turns a man's mouth into an echo of the vaginal lips: pink skin surrounded by shaggy, crinkly hair. And when the lips part, there is even the tongue to hint of the clitoris. The interplay of these visual sex games between vagina and mouth is even more fascinating when people shave their pubic hair off. Hairless, the female crotch is more like a mouth with a vertical smile. Hairless, the penis seems bigger. And what of the custom of men shaving? To remove hair from the face is in a sense to feminise it, and it is only balanced because now the male mouth is less like the vaginal lips – except when the vaginal hair has been shaved off.

Make love by stroking hair, removing pins, combs, bands. Ruffle the hair. Re-arrange it. Part it. Lift it from the neck, pull it over the face, and string it through the lips. There is enormous pleasure for both sexes in doing this and having it done.

As excitement mounts, nuzzle, stroke and twist the hair of the armpit between finger and thumb. Reach down and tussle the pubic hair, finding the flesh beneath. As sweat gets more copious, it trickles from the armpit along the armpit hairs. This dissolves the pheromones dried out on the hairs, making them volatile, and they do their work in the nose. Similar effects occur at the male pubis and the raised pubic hair of women.

After penetration, the pubic hairs glide over one another. Perhaps this is the explanation of the different shape since his thins at the top, and hers at the bottom. As he enters deeper, less friction is needed on the pubic hairs, and the shapes neatly fit that function. Have a look next time.

During oral foreplay, the male chin and cheeks with five o'clock shadow produces the bonus of slight friction on the upper part of the thighs. Her head hair caressing his penis head is pleasant because of the different textures. At orgasm the eyebrows get closer together in the short lived orgasmic frown. The eyelashes flicker with the quivering signal that peak tension and excitement has been reached. It is fitting that the eyes, which so often are the first thing we see in love, are also equipped with hairs – eyebrows and lashes – which in their own quiet, trembling way announce the climax.

There is in hair more than meets the eye, more indeed, as we have seen, than is touched or felt. It gives sensations by stimulating the part of the body it touches. Breasts respond well to being brushed with her own tresses or to being tickled on the nipples with tufts. But hair has its own sensitivity. At the base of the 100,000 hairs on the head, there are individual sense organs which respond to pressure so slight that they even give information about being brushed up the wrong way.

In the vast literature on sex, no mention has been given to the way hair relaxes after orgasm until now. The wild and bushy look gives way to the serene, easily managed tresses or curls of satisfied sex. During excitement, the penis, the clitoris, the nipples, all stand on end, and so does hair. After orgasm, they all lie down. Watch out for it; it only happens when everything has gone right.

Resolutions

TO MAKE an improvement in sex fun always means some sort of resolution, a change in attitude, a willingness to do something new. If you can make the resolve together, you have double the incentive. Once you make a resolution stick, you have a new era ahead of you for sexual fun. I've called these keep-fit exercises the New You Exercises – the new you and the new era of sex fun you enter.

Do these workouts together, and as you progress you will usually find that sexual expression is the natural end of exercising together. It's worth a try. In any case, the drill can help trim and shape you, which is always a bonus for sexual fun.

You'll find these exercises easy to do, and you can do most of them anywhere. Don't get bored by going into a heavy session. Start with a few minutes a day. Find your favourite one and do it when you feel the old you, tired and anxious, coming on.

A team of New York doctors have discovered that men are better lovers if they don't wear tight pants. Close fitting jeans restrict circulation, and make men too hot inside. A brisk swim – especially together – should set him up!

Real loving is very vigorous exercise, and can last a lot longer than a few minutes. Get ready to enjoy every minute with this regular exercise routine.

Relaxation

Stand in a relaxed manner, arms by your side, feet apart. Breathe in slowly, raising your arms to shoulder height at the same time. Then step forward as you complete breathing in.

In one easy, flowing motion, breathe out, lowering your arms as you do. Move your foot back to the standing position.

Do this several times in a very relaxed manner, first with the left and then with the right foot. Pay great attention to maintaining balance and control of your posture. Breathing should be gentle.

Once you get the idea, you can take a count of three to breathe in and a count of six to breathe out.

This exercise gives a good start to the day. It is excellent for relaxing the back and the shoulders.

What spot?

WOMEN SINCE time began have been having clitoral orgasm, vaginal orgasm, uterine orgasm. But modern pundits, according to the social and political climate, decree that there is only one valid orgiastic response. Currently, much attention is being given to the G spot. The G spot is actually an area rather than a specific location. It is found at the belly side of the vagina, just above the pubic arch.

What spot turns you on? The fun in sex can be enhanced if both partners look for those parts they are sure have been neglected. There is so much to explore, it takes years to map out the erotic territory in each body. Some sensitive areas require tricky anatomical precision to locate – but you may find them by happy trial and error, followed by practise.

Every type of orgasm occurs when a certain level of excitation is achieved, so you can see immediately that classifying the types is an ongoing activity, not a museum analysis.

What spot? Whichever brings orgasm and is not harmful.

Surprise

CULTIVATE IT, nurture it, plan it, hone up on it. One of the great benefits of having the same sexual partner is that you can be sure of ample opportunity for surprise, the reverse of familiarity and boredom.

He comes into the house and you unzip him and make him come: mouth, hand, vibrator, as you will. She is walking upstairs and you gently waylay and then lay. She is in the shower and you go in and penetrate her. He is asleep, so you make his penis rise and then sit on him and make him come.

The permutations are endless, the rewards infinite. If you've run out of ideas, simply flip through this book, find something you haven't done for a while, and do it now, wherever you are in the home turf.

CHUCKLES

Bottoms

THE BRITISH have bottoms, the Americans have asses and everyone has an arse. The words alone make you chuckle, and where there is a giggle, a smirk, or a belly guffaw, as well as a sweet smile like Mona Lisa's, sex is not far behind. Most studies of the bottom have been tongue in cheek, if I can use the pun.

One person in ten has a small, narrow bottom, and one in ten a huge, curvaceous bottom. Three men and women out of ten have very muscular ones, while the other 50 per cent of the population have bottoms that are balanced in the amount of fat and muscles.

During the development from child to adult, the bottom changes dramatically and rapidly, though this occurs earlier in girls than boys. During the years 12 to 14, a girl's bottom may increase 30 per cent in size, while ankles and wrists barely alter. Both sexes grow more anal hair, but in girls the anal skin is often peachier and smoother than in boys.

The change in the unisex, pre-adolescent bottom to the mature form occurs through the stimulus of sex and growth hormones. The latter widen the hip bones of females, but the initiation of the change and the shape depend on sex hormones. In males, the increase of width is not so dramatic, though the bones become stronger.

In both sexes there is an increase of muscle, but in the female there is a very marked deposition of soft fatty tissue. This results in a plumper, more curvaceous contouring of the skin over the fat, which rests on the muscles beneath.

Simultaneous with these changes into adulthood are genital development, though they take three to four years to be completed. The fact that the onset of sexuality is so clearly announced by bottom changes – shape and curve in the girl, hard muscle development in the boy – firmly establishes the bottom as an important feature of sex.

Walk down any street, particularly in summer, and you can see some enticing and instructive sights behind people. Women literally waggle their bottoms, the cheeks going at least two inches to the left and then to the right. Men don't. Few men have bottoms wider than their shoulders, while at least one woman in two does. Men go straight up from the hips, women go in curvily.

These basic facts arise out of sex differences, naturally, but why? Women waggle because their legs are set at an angle to their spinal columns. Men's are in the same straight line, so they don't have to keep correcting their balance to the same extent. This waggle serves as a sexual signal, a statement of what sex you are.

Women are wider in the hips relative to size because the bottom is built onto the pelvic girdle (a hula hoop fixed to the backbone) and this hoop has to be wide enough to allow a child's head to pass through during birth.

But why should a woman's bottom go in at the waist?

First, when copulating from the rear, the curving in of the hips gives the male something to hold on to for hard thrusting. If there had been two prototypes among our ancestors, one a straight-up-and-down woman and the other curvy as she is today, then it doesn't need much analysis to see who would be more attractive and popular.

Second, a curvy bottom means a curvy hip, and that provides a very cosy ledge to sit baby on.

All well and good, but the differences do not end there. A woman's bottom is fleshier than a man's. Even slim women have a good pinch of fat there. Furthermore, her bottom sags in comparison to a man's. Look at a female bottom side view. Be she ever so svelte, her rump has a softer, more fruity line to it. Part of the reason for this is shock absorption: our ancestors would use the monkey position, straight in from behind.

So ingrained are these sexual implications of the bottom's shape that women persistently report in sexual surveys they like tight, neat, small male buttocks. Large buttocks on a man confuse gender.

Women have two dimples, one on the top of their buttocks just above the cleavage of the buttocks, and another about three inches either side of the backbone. These sacral dimples are rare in men. Women who are sexually active seldom seem to lose these dimples, an observation I seem to be the first to have made. These dimples are also extremely sensitive. Tickle one and see.

Bottom skin is coarser than the back or the belly, but it is more varied. The cheeks themselves have the toughest skin, rapidly becoming more silk-like as the cleavage is approached. Inside the cleavage, hair is often sparser, and the skin is always silkier. Then it abruptly changes into very thin, delicate skin, the mucous producing variety of the anal orifice. In the relaxed state, the orifice displays an area of skin the size of a ten pence, very similar to vaginal lip skin and to the tip of the penis. It is just as sensitive.

The skin on the buttocks does not contain many sweat glands, but around the anus are many glands producing a musky aroma. This differs from person to person and ethnic group to ethnic group. Blacks produce a more pungent oil than whites, while fish-eating Japanese smell of the salt air to western noses.

When lovers stand face to face and begin embracing, his hands slide naturally down from the slippery waist on to her buttocks. Nine times out of ten, he will hold one cheek in each hand and lift. This opens the cleavage and activates two responses. Either there is a relaxation of the buttocks, in which case the pull of his hands translates to her vaginal lips, massaging them without touching them. Or, if she is less relaxed, she will tighten her buttocks. This signal is unmistakable – she isn't interested.

Kissing and fondling the breasts of a woman who is attracted to her prospective lover always results in buttock relaxation. The flood of warmth is intense, and as the penis engorges, the male's buttocks contract. So his is an exact opposite response. The reason is that the more relaxed she is, the more easily entered, and the tighter he can clamp his buttocks, the more blood there is available to fill the penis shaft. Tight buttocks then, so often mentioned by women as attractive, are more than just show: they imply potency.

Bottom muscles, glutends, are the largest muscles in the body and the most obvious physical feature from the back. Why? We get a clue by examining our nearest relatives, monkeys and gorillas. For all their bulk, gorillas do not have a correspondingly large pair of buttocks, nor do female monkeys and apes. The reason is that we walk upright, and having inherited the same basic skeleton as the apes, modification was necessary to make us upright.

Upright posture means we are able to use our hands and eyes better than apes, but a primary sexual display has been partially lost. The apes have highly coloured bottoms, and of course the sexual parts are clearly visible as they scamper about on all fours. Women from behind, when standing, are neatly discrete and colouration in both male and female is muted. To make up for these outward signs, sexual attraction has been centred on size and line. The bulk of the buttocks and the curve of the cheeks provide powerful sexual stimuli. Artists from antiquity to the present, especially modern photographers, have been obsessed with female contours, and the buttocks get their fair share of this interest.

Another difference between male and female bottoms is the thigh gap, which in some women is nearly five centimetres wide. This gap between the lower parts of the cheeks can be seen from the back. It is rare in men. It helps sexual penetration and arises from the wider set of women's leg bones.

When a woman bends down, she reveals her vaginal lips, and the colour is so strikingly different from the rest of the bottom that the effect is dramatic. The vaginal lips, which are bluish to dark red in the unexcited state, become pink to crimson in excitation, contrasting with the yellow, black, or cream-pink buttocks around them. When a man bends down, he affects women onlookers strongly because there, clearly suspended, is the scrotal sac. It is a curiosity of sexology that flashers are frontal displayers, not bottom showers. If they were serious about their sexual intentions, rather than being rather sad misfits of the sexual sideshow, they would use the more powerful back flash.

There is a minor industry producing clothes for boudoir fun which emphasise bottoms. Tights with cheek cut-aways, backless skirts, knickers opening from the back, gowns providing entrance at the rear. The straight tops of stockings make derrieres seem even more curved. Human ingenuity leaves evolutionary artwork behind.

When entering from the rear, his hands can slide up and over her bottom and slide naturally to her breasts. When entering from the front, his hands can slide from the breasts down to the buttocks. This provides touch stimulus to both, and she can encourage ardour by grasping his cheeks. Mouth and bosom: an echo of vagina and two bottom cheeks? Clearly, bosom and bottom reinforce each other as sexual force generators. They are not substitutes nor in competition.

The bottom's hemispheres, unlike the nipples or the lips, require considerable pressure in sex. In order to make her point with her lover's cheeks, a woman has to knead the flesh firmly to drive him harder into her. He must press his fingers deep into her buttocks to cause her to open more. Useful reflexes indeed.

In normal love play, anything can happen – and usually does sooner or later. High spirited lovers smack each other's bottoms, nibble them, knead them. As stimulus goes on, the man's muscles get tighter, hers looser. Sadism and masochism? No. No harm is done and intercourse is led into smoothly.

Anal sex offers interesting sidelines and diversions, and women can enjoy it; but it has to be learned because otherwise tissues can be split. The secretions of the anus are similar to vaginal secretions. Orgasms can result, and they are of a particularly deep and powerful kind, not as quick as clitoral orgasm. But the anus is a waste opening, and plunging from there into the vagina can result in severe infection, so care is needed.

Women whose lovers are on the wane can inject some life by smacking them on the bottom with the flat of the hand as they lie on their belly. Also, if she traces her finger down his spine into the bottom cleavage and finds the little tail there, she can increase his libido by stroking gently up and down on this point. Men can do the same for their women. Care is needed however, because this tail is very easily broken.

During missionary-position sex, she can knead his bottom and he hers. The most effective potency stimulus is for her to press straight into his bottom, while to get her full relaxation, he should open and close her bottom cleavage.

Once intercourse is away, there will be better stimulation if she tightens her bottom as he withdraws and relaxes as he enters. He in turn should tense his buttocks as he goes in, relax as he comes out. These are the most basic tunes you can play. Accomplished lovers write whole symphonies on this theme.

As his orgasm approaches, his relaxation and constriction proceeds automatically and at a faster rate. Hers do too. It is at orgasm that the bottom comes fully into its own, opening and shutting in rhythmic ripples.

The sex reflexes of the bottom are there to be used, as I have described. Once stimulated, they automatically give pleasure, operating as naturally as the blink of your eye or the swelling of sexual tissue under caresses.

Exercise

EVERY PERSON over about the age of 20 begins to suspect they need more exercise. In most cases this is a correct diagnosis. Nowhere is physical ability more important or more rewarding than in sex. The body must be capable of doing the things that give pleasure. But immoderate exercise is counterproductive.

The jarring spectacle of President Carter collapsing during an accelerated jog confirmed many anti-exercise lounge lizards' opinion: strenuous exercise is not only boring and uncomfortable but also dangerous. This has some truth in it.

Between 1968 and 1977 there were 56 sudden deaths in the British Army, that is, death within 24 hours, after strenuous physical exertion. These men died from heart and arterial breakdowns. They were all on active service and, up to the death, were professional soldiers. The basic health condition of people outside this stringent physical environment is likely to be inferior. The risk run is obvious.

Games like Rugby, football, and water polo involve periods of low activity with bouts of supreme exertion. Hitting a tiny soft tennis ball needs short explosive movements when volleying and trying to reach a serve. Running or jogging, although not intense, is strenuous exercise when prolonged. Sprinting uses maximum energy, calling up heart rates of 180-plus beats a minute.

Consequently, exercise cannot adequately be graded as severe or light, since both intensity and duration are involved. The sports that killed the soldiers were Rugby, football, cycling, weightlifting, hard route march, long distance running, circuit training.

Sexual intercourse involves duration and intensity, so learn to walk before you run. One can only conclude that the present fad for excessive jogging will be drastically re-appraised. Walk-ins, not run-outs, are not only safer, but more sociable: you can have a pleasant conversation during a ramble, and that relieves the dreadful tedium and discomfort of the run.

Horse riding

I WAS told in Epsom, where many successful jockeys live in large houses with large wives, that riding a horse makes a man capable and randy. I have also been told that riding a horse makes a woman adventurous, randy and energetic. In Epsom, there are streets where small bandy men hurry home after a race in new Jaguars, dart in quickly, and are not seen again until the next morning. Riding horses therefore appeared a possibility for sex fun.

The sheer act of sitting astride these curvy creatures and then being bobbed up and down ensures excellent toning of the perineum in both sexes. For women there is the added delight of labial and minor clitoral massage. Circulation is also improved – a must for sex – while the muscles of the thighs are strengthened. This enables thrusts of the required power for the man, and gripping dexterity for the woman. Couples who would have sex fun should try riding when at a loose end.

It is important to wear the right gear. In *Lancet* magazine, cases of thigh frost-bite were reported, but only in women. The learned physicians debating the case in the medical publication could not understand why women alone were so afflicted. Doubly a problem, because women have more insulating fat on the thigh than men, so one would have supposed a reversal of incidence in the sexes. However, the explanation was simple, they concluded. Women riders often wear tights, which are very thin. Men usually wear something thicker. A case for twill jodphurs or woollen tights for women, clearly.

Jogging

THE ONLY people whose sex lives improve through jogging are those so fit that they don't need to jog. When these fine physical specimens jog, they return flushed with hot blood. In sportive mood, they can make love. Other lesser, and much more numerous, mortals return from jogging in a state of shock. A dose of brandy, an aspirin and a warm bed with a hot-water bottle are infinitely more probable, and beneficial, than lovemaking.

There have been reported cases of penile frost-bite and attacks by pre-rabid dogs. Mess from pavement turds, the smell of petrol fumes from perineum to scalp, watering eyes – none are aphrodisiac even to the wilder fringes. Jogging, however, can be used as an aid in one circumstance – that of a chuckle. You both dress up in warm woollies – or in summer strip down to outrageous pants and vest – then go for a jog. Exhibitionism and a sense of togetherness are the keynotes here, as you brave the aforementioned dogs and rapacious motorists. As soon as ankles sag, or breath is short, you get back home and bath. The humour of the situation, the absurdity of it all (antelopes in the city) soon brings a glow of intimacy and the balm of shared rigours. And so to bed.

Weight training

USING WEIGHTS of iron, or machines especially constructed to progressively increase the amount of effort you have to move, is, bizarre as it may seem, a scientific study in its own right. Through the application of simple principles, just about any muscle or set of muscles can be selectively worked on. You and your lover may find the atmosphere of jock straps and straining brassieres to your taste. Try it, if you have done nothing together.

Body building is an esoteric, even arcane, past-time. It is usually taken up by adolescent youths aspiring to be like Tarzan. Nowadays, however, many women go in for it too. The point about it all is that you put on huge amounts of muscular tissue. When you work these muscles with weights, they become engorged. Indeed, a professional body builder is like a giant, be-veined, erect phallus. The effect in women is less evident, but still there. Masochism is given full play. The brute encounter with iron gives the psyche something to grapple with. Afterwards, sexual activity is a much sought relief.

Try it, if you want something really far out, but beware of becoming addicted. Too many weight trainers of the over-developed class seem to get their kicks out of self-love, while the erectile buzz of blood flushing into hypetrophied muscles may leave the hydraulics of phallus and labia wanting.

Swimming

SEA SWIMMING adds a glorious tang to the skin when you make love after. The chlorine of the local public baths is not aphrodisiac, but the exercise is. If you can use a private pool, do it buff and make love in the water. If nothing else, you learn what parts of you are buoyant.

River swimming in sylvan countryside, if you can find such, can entice sexual libidos made timid by domestic routine. Recommended.

Drinking

ALCOHOL, FOR those who like it, is a powerful aid for sex fun, but in excess it can be a dampener, if not of ardour, then of performance. Drinks make their effect through the pharmacologic action of ethyl alcohol on the hind brain, the part which controls many automatic functions, but alcohol also releases some inhibitive mechanisms. This last is important because constraints of up-bringing, social custom, even polite behaviour, are removed. Furthermore, alcohol can relax tense bodies. Clearly, then, here is a possibly potent aphrodisiac.

However, there are limiting factors in its use, and these must be well known in order to obtain the Dionysiac freedom the grape can bring, for it is wine rather than beer or spirits which induces the greatest amorousness. Beer is about 5 per cent or less pure alcohol, the rest being mainly water. Drinking this soon leads to a distended belly and the need for repeated visits to the lavatory, hardly conducive to love. Spirits such as scotch, bourbon and brandy are 40 per cent pure alcohol. The trouble with this high level of strength is that it is so easy to drink too much. Down the cocktails go, filling the stomach before they go to the head. And then, wham, you are over the limit, incapable of any coherent action or response. Wines, on the other hand, are intrinsically more nutritious, containing many minerals. They also have attractive smells, beautiful colours, and vary between about 8 per cent and 12 per cent pure alcohol. This means they can be drunk for pleasure as well as effect, more decorously than beer or spirits, and their effect on your cognitive processes are much more easily monitored.

From the stomach, alcohol passes into the small intestines and from both these organs diffuses into your bloodstream, which takes it to the brain. The higher the concentration in the blood, the more gets into your brain: hence the relationship between blood alcohol levels and degrees of inebriation. However, you lose alcohol from the bloodstream almost immediately through expired air in the lungs and in the urine. Consequently, a two-way flow is set up: what you drink and what you excrete. Some you actually burn up in the liver. The net result is that if you drink fast, you will overpower your regulatory functions and may end up dead drunk – in a coma, which is in no way different as far as your brain is concerned, or anyone else around you, from other narcotic comas. Indeed, people can die after drinking too much. For example, a full bottle of scotch drunk quickly on an empty stomach, and absorbed, will kill most people. Most, however, can handle a bottle a day, sipping a little at a time.

What all this means is that you can drink a bottle of strong wine over a three hour period and not be legally drunk. If you drink it in about an hour, you will most certainly be legally drunk. You can easily calculate the effect of spirits by figuring that you will still be coherent after one third of a bottle drunk in three hours. Three pints of beer can be taken in three hours.

These figures apply to a medium sized non-obese man of about 70 kilograms. For women, the effects are greater from these quantities for two reasons: first, because they are on average lighter than 70 kilograms and secondly because there seems to be an inbuilt quicker response rate in women as compared to men.

When men drink about half enough to be drunk, their libido rises and they can perform extremely well. When drunk, however, they are poor lovers – indeed, impotent. Women actually can enjoy sex even when drunk, so the gentleman owes it to his partner to drink less than she does. A caring male lover will withhold the fourth glass of wine from his lips, while liberally pouring her another.

Having got the biochemistry out of the way, what are the implications for sex fun between people of a long standing and affectionate relationship? Simple: invest in a wine cellar.

There is no need to break the bank, but some discrimination is necessary. French wines for example should only be purchased with the 'Appelation Controlée' statement on the label. German wines, like Spanish and Greek wines, have much to offer too, but be sure to buy recommended brands – some are concoctions of alcohol, dye and water from a chemical factory. There is absolutely no mystery in all this. Today you can buy perfectly good wines from established supermarkets, at very modest prices. Californian wines are also excellent value. Here is a short, rather personal list:

Valpolicella and Classico two to three years old, fruity and mellow, good with almost any European dish. New Beaujolais during the summer, a marvellous lover's wine as appealing to women as men. Spumante – sweet, but when cold and fresh, so light and weak that much can be drunk without inducing the sleepy stage. Graves, Sauternes, Moselles are among my favourites. Each wine has its own amorous effect, so experiment to find those that titillate you both. And remember, if you like red and your lover white, never use half bottles; an opened bottle will keep till tomorrow.

Movements for pleasure

CURIOUS AS it may seem, many couples lose out on sex fun not so much because they do not like each other or sex, but because they have lost the art of enjoying movement. Since you cannot do much in sex without moving, the curiosity is not so much that it happens, but that they allowed it to happen.

Fortunately, the situation can be remedied very easily, and I will give some simple exercises, which really do work, after explaining the background to the pleasure of movement. Do the exercises together, naked, in a warm room or on a warm night.

Movement itself is pleasant. Swimming, walking, dance, all give pleasure, and therefore we must conclude they affect hormonal levels. Certainly when competition is involved, the experience becomes exhilarating, and this is related to acute rises in adrenalin levels. The more serene, deeper pleasure of balanced bodily activity is not mediated by adrenalin, but by endorphin and encephalin (hormones from the brain), since it is a question of mood in harmony with leisurely movement.

Stress removes pleasure hormones, and so direct action is required to remove stress and to stimulate production of pleasure hormones. For many years now I have taught an array of relaxing, pleasure-giving movements, much modified from yoga, Tai Chi and dance forms. They work. They work well before going to bed, they work well in the morning. Their efficacy has been outstandingly demonstrated in groups of women who, tired and even stressed from a day's work, soon wipe out these effects by pleasure in movement. I have identified some movements which activate the pleasure balance of the body.

Endorphin and Encephalin stimulating movements

Alpha Get on all fours, knees about one foot length apart, on a soft surface, gently curve the back down and make the belly almost touch the floor. Gently push your breath out as if you were whistling, and when totally exhausted, gently but firmly pull your belly in as you breathe in and bend your back up. Hold for a count of three, then 'whistle' for total exhalation as you let your back sag again. Repeat in your own rhythm, gently, firmly, and take note of the pleasurable feelings. Repeat at least ten times.

Beta Lie on your back, hands at side, palms face down, legs bent at the knees, feet about two foot lengths apart. As you breathe in, press on hands and feet to raise hips from the floor. Breathe in gently as you raise your hips steadily, taking at least five seconds. Hold your breath for a count of five, then exhale by the 'whistle' method, taking at least ten seconds to exhale completely as you bring your bottom to touch the floor again. Note the pleasurable feelings. Repeat at least 12 times, developing your own rhythm, to give you maximum pleasure. Make it gentle.

Thighs

THE SKIN on the inside of the thigh between the legs is thinner than the outer sides. There are more sense organs here too, and they appear to get more numerous nearer the crotch. This is why caresses from the knee up get more delicious, in both sexes.

These sensitive areas are versatile. They can detect wetness, dryness, feel the difference between fingers and tongue. They respond to pressure and to warmth. Obviously this area is a major turn-on zone, suitable for much exploration. Waves of stimulation can be kept up by kissing, licking, nibbling gently, gradually ascending at the same time as stroking. As one caress ends, say with the mouth, the other can begin with the finger tips. The penis is particularly effective here, because the rougher shaft skin is an enticing contrast with the moister, smoother head. Because the skin is so velvety smooth on a woman's inner leg, the pleasure is reciprocal. Women use the nipple to pleasure the man.

Certain specialised sweat glands near the crotch produce substances which are in themselves turn-ons. They are found in men and women, but often extend further down in women. This is one of the reasons why oral sex is a turn-on for both the one doing it and the subject of it. Too much soap and use of deodorants kills the fun. For lovemaking, warm baths an hour or two before and a good rub down give the thighs a chance to secrete their natural scents. Why not encourage it?

Women still wear stockings when they are making a special effort for a romantic interlude. Indeed, as a lover's hand comes up from the knee, tracing the hose along, both get the pleasure of touch. But getting tights off at the crucial time can spoil the moment. They are useful work-day garments, not so good for romance.

The average woman – one in two – has a thigh circumference at the crotch of about 60 centimetres. Larger women might have thighs of 5 centimetres more without being fat, slim ones about 5 centimetres less. The length of the thigh is nearly 1½ feet, but this does not contribute to height because the thigh bone – the longest single one in the body – is set at an angle and is jointed above the crotch. So although a person may have an inside leg measurement of 53 centimetres – longish for an average woman and about medium for an average man – the true length of the leg is greater.

Men's thighs come straight down and are parallel, but women's are at an angle. It is this slope that gives women their very definite shape, curving in from the hips. And because women have very small waists in comparison to men's, the effect is even more pronounced. Women are broad in the thigh in comparison to the rest of their bodies – hence the American term 'broads'.

Viewed from the side, women's thighs have an outward

curve at about crotch level. A man's lines are straighter. Slide your hand over your hip bone. If you are a man, you'll find there is little curve to take you to the crotch, but if you are a woman, your hand will sweep naturally along the lines of the body, over and down to where thigh and tummy join. Once in this gully, the progress is natural to the vagina. Try it on one another.

From the back, the thighs lead to the buttocks. A woman caressing a man frontally finds that his lines guide her on to the penis, and a man caressing a woman soon finds his fingers naturally in the gap between the thighs at the top. But both sexes caressing from behind find that the hand goes between the legs, inwards. Try it.

In foreplay love games, the thighs are not to be missed. Many women have such a strong response that stroking the outside and gradually working to the inside can build up such excitement that a reflex action makes the thighs part. Women have explained how a good lover will not always open their legs, nor will they themselves open them, until they actually experience a tugging of the outer muscles and a relaxation of the inner ones.

These inner muscles are so strong that few people have the power to prise the legs apart in an unwilling partner. This obviously has a protective function and is why rape is usually accompanied by brutality or threats.

The thigh muscles in men must also be able to tense and relax, according to the job demanded of them. Often men with sexual problems, particularly the inability to gain or sustain an erection, have very poor tone in the thigh. Masturbation in both sexes is much more satisfying if the thighs are flexed and relaxed.

Strong thighs mean that women can cradle their lovers well. Strong thigh muscles are important in sex for men because the thrust and withdrawal motions depend on them. This is true in nearly every sexual position. And the same workout occurs in women, though different parts of the thigh are used. The most powerful counter thrustings a woman can make are reached when her feet are flat, her knees bent. Greater depth of orgasm is achieved when pushing in this position is interspaced with stretching the legs full out and wide and pushing with the pelvis, the weight on the heels. She has to be fit to do that, but it builds up greater and greater excitement. And a deep orgasm. By varying the angle of the spread of her legs and where she puts her weight, a woman can more or less control how deep the man goes, and where the greatest pressure is sensed. This is important when lack of expertise in her lover means her clitoris is not getting stimulated. The thighs make the sighs – if they are used to control the angle of his thrust. This is easy to learn through experimentation.

As orgasm in woman approaches, there are waves of tensing and relaxing of the inner thigh muscles. This can be so strong that many men buckle under the pressure, as she sweeps her knees together and presses his legs together. This pressure has to be counteracted by his thighs. There is no doubt that women get deeper and better orgasms if they can press hard like this.

Many women complain that they can't use their strength. They don't put it like that. They say things like, 'I wonder if he can stand it, so I just give up', or 'Until I met my husband, most men told me to stop pressing; however, he's like the Rock of Gibraltar'.

Card games

THE OFT-praised strip poker offers little to those in sexual bliss, partly because poker is such an incredibly boring game, stripping notwithstanding. But bridge, canasta and rummy can all be used to make a sexual pay-off. For example, a canasta meld or bridge finesse can be paid off with slow masturbation, fellatio, cunnilingus, or whatever. There is something in the human mind which likes to anticipate a win and the prize. How much more exciting if the prize is sexual gratification instead of pennies and matches. Highly recommended with or without friends.

Chess

AN EXCRUCIATING game played by berserk Russians, schizophrenic Americans, and young English people who like Hastings. In sex fun, however, much glee can be derived from chess. The sexual overtones in this game are unmistakable – mating and all that – but the opportunities of blatant sexuality are manifold.

When you take her queen, insist on the most servile of sexual services from her. When you take his bishop, enlarge your whims of sexual power by turning the man into the pawn of your fancies. The possibilities are endless, and like the game, can go on evening after evening after evening. A splendid domestic sex ploy, this, highly and unreservedly recommended to all who like to exercise their brain cells during sex.

LAUGHS

Aromatic massage

THIS FORM of massage uses aromatic natural oils. The result is relaxation and an almost certain boost in sex fun.

Natural oils can pass through your skin, actually reaching your bloodstream. Once there, your heart pumps them around your body. Eventually they reach that part of you that other oils cannot reach.

Though Roman ladies in Nero's love feasts used such oils for beauty and sex, we have only recently begun to understand why. So powerful are they that scientists have investigated them closely. Evening primrose oil, for example, has been shown to improve eczema when taken in capsule form. Some of the most beautiful aromas in the world are found in natural oils. Think of rose, lavender, peppermint, pine, clove.

Aromatherapists believe that certain oils cure certain

ailments: parsley for anxiety, rosemary for muscular aches, rose for insomnia, and peppermint for sexual stimulation. These oils are made by pressing the plant to squeeze the juice out or by making special extracts, which are then concentrated. Natural aromas are so powerful that you can smell a peeled orange across a room.

As the oils are massaged into your skin, they also evaporate into the air, energised by the increasing warmth of your body. As your hands glide over your lover's body, friction is generated and creates heat; but, more important, touch dilates the blood vessels, sending more blood to the skin. The result is a heavenly combination of exquisitely pleasant aromas and warm caressing hands. As you sigh, you breath the vapours in, adding another dimension to sensual experience.

In sex, the major benefits come from the massage, the relaxation, the beautiful smells. Fortunately we know from many years of research what areas to touch to give bliss, so choose your massage oil and 'aromatise'!

You can start off using baby oil or lotion. Body rubs aren't as good as creams because they are a little astringent, but they usually have delightful aromas, so a combination of baby lotion and a body rub is a good way to begin. Massage the body rub in first and then follow up with baby oil or lotion. There are many good proprietary skin creams or body treatments. Shop around for the aroma you want.

Here are some good routines I've developed for self aromassage. They tone the muscles which shape your body, and they also relax you.

Pick any good body cream or ointment, one with a smell you like. A lighter ointment passes into dry skin more easily, heavier oils and creams into greasy skins more easily. Most blond people have dry skin, most dark haired, greasy.

Plan the massage for just after the shower, before you go out, or before you go to bed. Body creams pass into your skin easily, so there is no mess; but experiment at first so you don't use too much.

A really good relaxer is to use your fingertips, with some ointment on them, using a very gentle circular motion about 5 centimetres from the navel, with the navel as the centre of the circle.

Another good toner in aromassage is to cream your palms and lay your hands flat on each side of your legs, just below the hips, and stroke upwards to the waist. Keep doing it until the oil or cream has disappeared into your skin.

For him to do for you and for you to do for him: Lie on a soft rug on a long beach towel on your back with oils and ointments ready. He kneels by you on your right side. He puts the oil in the palm of his hand – a small amount at first until he gets the hang of it – and then in slow, gentle, pressing strokes he starts at the elbow and works up the arm, over the shoulder, to the neck, very very gently. Then he repeats it until all the oil has gone into your skin. Taking some more oil, he then softly massages along your belly with strokes up to the breast (keeping off the navel). By this time you will be very, very relaxed, all your tension gone. He then kneels on your left side and repeats the whole process. Then you turn over and he works on your buttocks, stroking up to the head.

Returning the favour for him can be difficult, because many men are so hairy. But it's worth trying.

Pleasure points

NOT JUST the old erogenous zone idea, but a much more penetrant understanding of the sexuality of the body based on acupuncture points. Acupuncture asserts that certain small regions of the skin are direct stimulants of the sexual mechanism. Luckily, you do not have to stick needles into one another because any stimulation of the given points will do. For fun sex you pinch them, scratch them with your fingers, press them with your penis, nipples, thumb or little finger, nibble them, kiss them, or lick them. Here are the recommended points: The area 5.5 centimetres below the navel. The area 2.5 centimetres directly above the navel and the two areas 2.5 centimetres on either side of the navel. The line from the crotch down to the knee on the inside of the thigh. The centre of each buttock, but not *between* the buttocks.

A 'point pirouette' is good fun. One of you lies down in a spread eagled position, draped with a cloth – the more sumptuous the better. A bottle of wine is opened, and music is played. The drape is pulled off, and each point on the front of the body mentioned above is gently stimulated with a fingertip. A glass of wine is then drunk, after which all the back points are stimulated. Another glass of wine is drunk. The front points are stimulated again, this time using tongue, nipple or penis. Another glass, a repeat on the back.

Saunas

THESE ARE well worth installing in your home, since these days they are relatively cheap. Public saunas have strange lingering smells, which do not aid sex.

In your own cosy sauna you can sit and perspire nicely. Don't make the mistake of having sex in there. The heat stress alone is sufficient for your body to cope with, even if young. The delicious feeling of relaxation that comes in a sauna induces pleasurable sensations over the whole body, particularly in the nether regions. As soon as the sexual temperature is right, go into a warm place and make love.

To use a mechanical simile: the sauna affects the body and its sexual powers rather like the way warming up a racing engine affects the car's performance – it changes gear better, it goes faster and it doesn't wear out so easily.

Showers

HAVING SHOWERS together provides aquatic opportunity for many ploys, most rewarding in their sensual content. As the water streams down, you sponge each other off, giving each other intimate washes, and all mental blocks are washed away. Once the soaping and rinsing is over, he can stand behind her and, using the water as lubricant, massage belly, breasts, thighs, and the paradise gate. Soon his phallus rises and inveigles naturally behind her. Let love then take its course.

You can start with her behind him instead massaging chest, belly, thighs, and enticing his manhood out. Fans of sex in the shower talk of the raptures of making oral love in streaming water. There is also mention of the actual sound of the shower, reminiscent of a lover's tryst on a rainy day.

Showers are surely worth exploring. The change of texture in skin and hair are aphrodisiac, while the wholesome aromas that rise from the freshly showered body are another bonus. But take care not to use too much soap. The membranes of the sex organs are easily denuded of protective secretions if soap is used heavily, leaving them too fragile for prolonged friction.

Body bouquets

RESEARCH HAS shown that smell hormones, called pheromones, are simple fatty acids and flavours. Some are found in fruits. Body bouquets certainly can be changed by what you eat.

The obvious smell of horses is caused by hippuric acid. We make this acid in our livers when we change food additives into it. Unfortunately, some of these unwanted substances are found in processed foods, with the result that you get a body bouquet that you could do well without – unless you belong to the horsey set.

The other easy to understand factor in body bouquet is the skin, which harbours natural yeasts and bacteria, all perfectly harmless. In fact, they kill off germs. But they also change perfumes because they eat perfumes. This is why you should try out a scent for several hours at least: your body will change the actual chemistry of that perfume.

Some people have natural yeasts which can turn even the most ordinary soap odour into ravishing perfume. Other people can metabolise the most expensive perfume and come out smelling like an alley cat.

Bouquets from foods and drinks

Garlic and Onion. If you want to he happy with this bouquet, both of you should eat them at the same time. In some people, garlic odour is present 36 hours after a meal, coming from the skin in the sweat. Chemically, these smells are related to that in the oils the skunk makes, the mercaptans, some of the most malodorous in existence.

Beetroot. These contain skatole, a substance found in faeces.

Processed food. Most is neutral for body bouquet, but look at the label for benzoate. It gives you that horsey smell.

High-fat foods and those with large amounts of butter

When fresh, butter smells wonderful, but when rancid, it smells of feet. This is because butyric acid is formed. Animal fats tend to contain butyric acid.

If you want to smell like a cow, eat a lot of beef; like a sheep, eat a lot of mutton; like a herring, eat a lot of fish. We actually stockpile the fat from these foods under our skin. We need some fat, but eat about four times too much of it, so improve body odour by cutting down on it.

Beer produces a bitter body bouquet because of the hops. Liqueurs and wines have minute quantities of persistent perfumes which come through the skin. For a heavy, romantic bouquet, it's worth buying a bottle of good French red the night before. White wines, especially German, yield a more light-hearted body bouquet.

A glass of Green Chartreuse imparts an exotic bouquet – a cool-breeze odour with fire underneath. Tia Maria – gives a long, lingering, warm bouquet. Experiment with others. But beware of cheap liqueurs. Their body bouquet will be cheap too.

Sexy bouquet – for him

You can get a fresh, enticing smell with salads and still more salads. Chlorophyll in salad greens is the great freshener, but it doesn't kill the underlying masculinity. Salads give you that irresistible country-fresh, wide-open-sky smell and with the strength of the earth in it. For the dressing, cut up grapefruit peel and press it into the oil with the flat of a spoon. And add thyme.

Sexy bouquet – for her

The fragrance of flowers with an undercurrent of sauciness: you get it from salads. Lettuce, cucumber, carrots and tomatoes provide the freshness. The sauciness comes from the herbs you mix in.

Rosemary is tart and fresh, basil a little sharper. Lemon juice adds a clean odour to your skin, while orange adds warmth. Go easy on vinegar, but cut up orange peel and lemon peel and press into the oil.

The body bouquet diet

Breakfast. Bright fresh smells to start the morning: orange juice, lemon juice, grapefruit juice, or a whole orange cut in four or half a grapefruit. Cereal: shredded wheat, all-bran, bran flakes, or rolled oats with raisins and milk to taste (skim the fat off first). To add aroma to cereal, slice a banana on top. Fresh coffee – not instant – is one of the best smells around. There are also some lovely scented teas, but they are expensive; a good cuppa is fine for fragrance anyway.

Elevenses. Kiwi fruit: these beautiful green fruits with a furry skin are really delicious and have a delicate lime-like smell. Or try an apple, orange, cherries, plums. Taken with your coffee, these fruits can really sweeten your day.

Lunch. Starter: melon with ginger – now there's a good-smell combination – or half an avocado pear with one teaspoon of sunflower or safflower oil, sprinkled with mixed herbs. Yoghurt is good, too. When fresh it has a really breezy smell, and it is digested so easily that you keep the fresh smell.

Main course: sandwiches made with wholemeal brown bread and vegetable oil margarine is a good basis: Fill with all the salads you like except beetroot, garlic, radishes and onions, and top with cottage cheese. You can have up to three of these without worrying about the calories. Alternatives are salt beef and boiled carrots or boiled greens, or a really fresh fish grilled or boiled.

Sweet: Finish off with fruit – pineapple, cherries, plums, apples, pears, alone, or made into a salad by just peeling, dicing and mixing in their own juice. You don't need cream, but a little yoghurt will answer nicely.

Tea-time. As Elevenses.

Evening meal. Here's a romantic, sweet-smelling, spoil-yourself menu, happily low on calories.

Open up a good bottle of red wine and let it breathe – this means it gets to smell fresher and fresher. If you like white wine, keep it chilled.

Starter: chop up five sticks of celery, boil in one pint of water, add half a chopped green pepper and sprinkle with mixed herbs and black pepper. By the time the soup is cooked, it will be just enough for two small but wonderful-smelling servings. All vegetable soups made with fresh vegetables, except leeks, onions and garlic, smell good but greens have to be really fresh.

Main course: cauliflower cheese (absolutely fresh cauliflower and mild cheddar cheese), or ham with boiled courgettes and new potatoes sprinkled with parsley.

Sweet: Finish off with a miniature liqueur each.

Holidays

NEW SCENERY, new places, new people – all can help give freshness to your sexuality, especially if you have children and can arrange to take a holiday without them. The key to using your holiday for enriching your sexuality is to go for that express purpose. This means that guided tours are out. You will be too regimented for spontaneity and so tired from trekking from one sight to the next that you will fall exhausted into your bed at night. Go on your own.

Choose a good hotel, the best you can afford. One with room service is essential so that you can have meals and anything else you fancy without going out and whenever you feel like it.

Warm climates are more conducive to sex than cold. You can spend many hours sunning, swimming, or walking slowly about. Take sufficient exercise to invigorate but not tire yourself.

Because you are being waited on hand and foot, you have little else to think about but your next spell of lovemaking. You can exploit the hotel's sauna, get a rub down, and rest, rest, rest from the daily domestic round.

Serious sex funsters will be careful not to become embroiled in a time wasting round of casual parties and cocktails with chance acquaintances. It may be pleasant, but will make inroads into your sex time. You have gone away to explore your sexuality together. It is a full time occupation. On holiday, you will have the opportunity of using your best energies for sex, when and how you like, uncurtailed by work and domestic demands.

Positions

A SUBJECT nowadays not so much of fun but of boredom. Despite earnest compilations, often citing a gross or more of positions in intercourse, the case can be accurately summed up by the sage who said: 'There are only two positions, in and out'.

But perhaps that really puts it too simply. If you do not know position variations after several years of caring cohabitation, you should. It is wise to keep a diary of the positions you use over ten sets of intercourse. If you use only one basic one, whatever that may be, you either have a vigour in it that is unbeatable, or you have lapsed into ennui. A poll among my couples revealed that the actively sexual use a core of some half dozen positions, scrambled as the mood takes them.

An historical note: the missionary position is said to be the woman on her back and the man on top of her. Actually, it was the woman on her knees, kissing his foreskin while he stood patting her head in yearning benediction.

Having kept the diary, the two of you can then tick off the positions according to each one's satisfaction as to reception, penetration, orgasm, comfort, and so on. Having so classified them, you next codify them as A, B, C, and so forth. Then you can write out choreographies for sex: A, 2 minutes; B, 30 seconds; C, 3 minutes, or as you will. You perform these choreographies on certain love-feast days, anniversaries, birthdays. You can take it in turns to write the choreographies

An interest in music can add a new dimension. For example, would you be up to choreographing Beethoven's Fifth or the uninhibited 'Freude! Freude!' choral of his Ninth? What about your favourite rock tune? The legendary Ravel's *Bolero* is unmercifully boring the second time around, but its syncopation and repetition is great for young lovers the first time.

Music

IF YOU are young enough not to know Ivor Novello's romantic music, try the nostalgia trip during sex by using cassettes or records of his memorable tunes. For some, there may be honeyed bliss to be had from Mantovani's humming strings. Musical taste is individual: one couple uses John Wesley's hymnal. Not so strange if you remember that Protestant non-conformists were noted for their large families. Hymn singing is actually a great rouser of the sexual instinct.

Today's gadgetry allows each lover to choose the music he or she responds to. Both can have separate sound systems. She wears earphones from hers, he from his. Both tune in, get turned on – and lovemaking proceeds without offending either's ears. It's worth a try to switch headgear around half-way through to find out if you really are in tune with each other.

Music pays off for any expense and study it requires to become part of sex fun.

Furniture

IS THERE a piece of furniture in your home which has not figured in your sexual adventures? If so, bring it into play at once.

The majority of our couples have used everything in their houses: bidets, baths, ironing boards (make sure the iron is unplugged), divan, sofa, bar stool, pouf (the only time heterosexuals may legitimately have fun on a pouf), kitchen sinks.

Basically these are used for support, for lying on and over, for increasing tension in the back or arching bodies into more revealing and quiveringly vulnerable positions. The pouf and the big bean bag are superior in this respect. If he lies over one face down, he can be got at by her hand on his perineum, bottom, and scrotal sac. If he lies on his back, he can be given the exquisite treatment of fellatio or slow masturbation. For her, the same exciting possibilities exist.

Places

THERE IS not a spot in our sexually active couples' houses that has not been a witness or support of sexual conjugation. The stairs: fascinating possibilities of pursuit, great opportunities for involved geometrics. The cellar: a throwback to our cave-dwelling ancestors. The pantry: memories of childhood. The bathroom: cleanliness is next to lasciviousness. The kitchen: a meal wonderfully interrupted. The toilet: childhood notions of being dirty. The sitting room: when the boring guests have gone. The dining room: after an evening of playing footsie under the table during that obligatory party. It is beautiful how the memory lingers when the hum drum is transformed into the delectable.

Naturally, the world outside your home presents opportunities. Mutual masturbation under the large tablecloths of the Ritz dining room can take the fear out of the size of the bill. A grope in the back of a taxi – mobile sex – can deafen you to the traffic din. Train compartments are tantalising: you pull the blind down, and the brush with the danger of someone barging in makes lubricity as smooth as the old steam engine's pistons.

There is one taboo: don't indulge in sex when one of you is driving. An experienced motorway policeman told me that many drivers are in a state of undress when they crash.

The world is indeed your oyster – or if you prefer a homeopathic image, your mussel.

Roman dining

YOU ALREADY know that eating together is a pleasant introduction and prelude to sex, but there are limitations in the Western mode of sitting on chairs at a table. Try this: with cushions, mattresses, poufs and a low table, lounge about like Romans, feeding each other grapes, drinking your favourite wines. Intercourse can then act as course breaker.

Lubricants

THE BEST is just plain spit, but various water-based gels are available and these mix with the natural juices of the body. You'll both get more out of sheaths if he lubricates his penis first, and also the sheath. She'll get more out of his fingers if she helps with her spit. Sometimes the flow of vaginal juices uncannily stops at the vital moment. No need to panic. He can give you a long full-tongued kiss during which much fluid will pass to you.

Showing off

A MUST for all serious seekers of sex fun. There is no doubting the fascination men have for simply watching their lovers, but our reports show that few have exploited this costless amusement to their partners. Women were more reticent in divulging what they might get out of looking at their men. Clearly, then, this is an area for experimentation.

Try this. One lover watches the other undress, and then he or she lies naked in various revealing postures. These postures are retained for minutes at a time, so make sure you are both warm. The eastern mystics practised this kind of meditation as an elevated pathway to Nirvana. It works. Calm rather than frenzy encompasses the mind as a lover watches the contours, sweeps, valleys, textures and flanks of the partner. Gradually, this peace is warmed with the rosy tint of engorging labia or phallus as the pensive mind projects into the future joining of the two bodies.

So powerful is this method of sexual arousal, so huge are the energies imparted, that it is well worth trying. Do it in small doses, tracing the body with your eyes, letting the mind roam in this enchanted landscape (it is no accident that the human nude is a figure of both landscape and architecture at the highest level). You will find your breathing, soft and gentle, takes on the rhythm of your partner. Then the hands may explore what the eye has seen, then the tongue, and so on with increasing intimacy and trust, until you find you are in nexus – in a relaxed, refreshing way.

Sex clothes

DURING THE last ten years there has been a blooming of a new industry – the manufacture and selling of clothes designed specifically for eroticism and intended to be worn only in sexual encounters.

Freely advertised in the daily yellow press and Sunday heavies, the brochures usually have a premium charge. They are generally well produced in full colour.

Sociologically, the phenomenon of Sex Clothes is of great interest. As aids to sex fun, the attire is well worth a look, though at times the goods are rather expensive for what they are.

You two may have great fun merely by trying out your received opinions against the copy writer's blurbs. You can decide on whether or not to invest in a scorching nightdress –

yes, they call that 'hot stuff'. More exotic are the 'You Tarzan, Me Jane' clothes with printed leopard spots. This, we are promised, 'will have him purring with delight'. It is clear that in the Sex Clothes brochure world, men are mere receptors for sexual arousal, tamed or half frenzied according to the whim of his lady love when she wears the appropriate garment. There is no reason why the male shouldn't wear these garments for frissons of a transvestite nature.

Tights

MEN SEEM to have a love-hate response to tights. Indeed they produce cultural shock in men over 40, who are used to finding smooth skin above a stocking top. In younger men, the shock is absent – but so is the thrill. Tights, nevertheless, can be useful aides in sex fun.

Available for sex fun with open crotch, seamless or seamed, fishnet or silk-like, tights are cheap, colourful, and washable. Some brands have simulated suspenders built in. Others are available in a one legged style, allowing a mediaeval jester effect when a different hue is used on each leg.

Open-crotch tights have a following for good reason: the vulva is attractively displayed, and the contrast of textures to touch and eye, mouth and finger, is readily observed. For vigorous men, ordinary tights offer a challenge. One couple enact a sort of 'deflowering' of the garment itself. She wears new tights and lies on her back with legs astraddle. He attacks the gusset with his teeth to gnaw an entry for his phallus.

Whereas women's legs encased in tights provoke the libido, men wearing them promote laughter. This 'Nureyev syndrome' can bring much jollity to the boudoir. Perhaps a research team will discover why men wearing tights make women laugh. Since laughter breaks the ice, males intent on sex fun can announce their intentions in a way reminiscent of the troubadour by turning up in bedroom or salon (drawing room, lounge, kitchen) wearing nothing but tights. Since men's legs and knees are usually more gnarled and knobbly than women's and since the vigorous male soon strains the gusset beyond its elastic limit, his lady will have the benefit of a delightful shiver of expectation.

Stockings

THESE ARE essential ingredients of the lovers' wardrobe. Women experience a certain voluptuousness in wearing them, while men delight in the shape of their beloved's leg so enticingly enmeshed. We have reports of men near ecstasy over the way their beloved's tiny leg hairs peep through the mesh, and how, as the fingers slide up a seam and reach the stocking top, there is the delicious thrill of passing to skin. Cheap and attractive, stockings have the lover's imprimature, awarded the rosette of satisfaction.

Knickers

CROTCHLESS, BRIEF or briefer, plain white or satin red, silk or cotton – knickers provoke the libido like a red rag to the bull. They are worn to be taken off. Sex fun is enriched by the variety of texture, colour, and design of these inexpensive accessories. In combination with stockings, new worlds of enticement are explorable.

Suspenders and belts

FULLY TESTED, thoroughly tried sex aids, they can add a touch of the bordello or the refinement of an age past when gentlewomen wore these accessories. The benefits of dressing up in suspenders or belts was extravagantly praised by several men in our reports. There is something of the peeking-under-the-queen's skirt in all this. The lady, ritually adorned in stockings, suspenders, knickers, bra, is an all out sensual assault upon a man's sensitivities. She is a sex goddess, a queen of concupiscence, a Venus of venality, a lady of love.

The engorged male may not only kiss her toe, lick her stocking top, do obeisance to the thighs above the garment line, he may actually penetrate, for he is welcome. This is not, as some cynics would have us believe, a time of chivalry dead. Rather it is a time of domestic Camelot, where knights in their white bikini fronts rescue wifely damsels from the thrall of boredom by praising her charms and filling her grail. It is a day of Guineveres looking out from the kitchen battlements and espying a forlorn fellow who has been working with her for years to make a happy life, wilting under the ennui of daily commuter concourse. Together they rise above these petty greynesses into a magical world of sexual bliss where stockings and suspenders help them scale the battlements.

Shirts and pants

PANTS CUT in the continental style add spice to the early encounters of love. We are reliably informed by ladies who know that there is a libido releaser in the well filled front of a man's pants. It is akin to the impact on a man of the stockings, the bras, the suspender belts. Like them, these may be uncomfortable, but well worth putting up with to give your beloved her thrill.

Silk shirts, opened to reveal hair on the chest, engender notions of romance, even of the Gigolo. These susceptibilities can be raised to a higher pitch by a fragrant body spray.

Shoes

WOMEN HAVE a choice of so many styles that enormous variety is possible when shoes are worn with stockings, knickers and bra, as well as old summer frocks with a story to tell. Shoes should perhaps be the talisman or taliswoman of past encounters. A pair of old pumps worn in your courting days can be washed, whited, and hung over the bed as a reminder of your earliest attraction to each other.

Older men are in the main still zany about seamed stockings and high heeled shoes. You can also try sports shoes with knee length socks.

Men can try wearing old rugger boots, suitably immaculate, in an attempt to recapture the swish of the days when she watched you pull your groin for less rewarding reasons.

Socks

A MUCH neglected ploy. To wear socks is useful on cold nights, and they can be stripped off with some ceremony to reveal the pinkies. Foot fetishism has an endearing domesticity about it when employed like this. Socks up to the knee or halfway can add textural variety to touch, while men with a taste for give and take can wear sock suspenders. As a particularly male accessory, they could with sufficient exposure become as potent a libido releaser as women's suspenders. There is always the faint air of the ridiculous about this garment, and that presages good potential for sex fun.

Uniforms

SO POWERFULLY is our sexuality connected with embellishment that uniforms naturally have their place in sex fun. The beginning ideas are obvious enough: sixth form girl uniforms are a turn on for a majority of men. Astonishingly, one third of the women in our surveys had kept their fifth and sixth form uniforms, but very few men had kept their school blazers.

Ideas come hard and fast. She may get a thrill out of you in a police outfit, or as a sailor or a pilot. He may be elated to find you in a 1920 maid's outfit. Remember all the old milkman jokes? Why not try the milkman's striped smock and peaked cap? Give a thought to the lady traffic warden's dark serge and gold uniform.

Uniforms can be purchased cheaply if you keep your eyes open for small ads in the dailies or go to government surplus shops. You can hire anything you wish from a theatrical costumer, but this is far from cheap

What may be erected, or opened, by the donning of a Sam Browne? Are the couplings achieved by Chef and Waitress, Doctor and Nurse, Driver and Conductor fascinating to you? What about a grass skirt from Hawaii or a sarong from the South Pacific? If you are of an intellectual bent, read up on the sexual mores of the people whose style of dress you wear. This provides further scope for invention, since sexual desire is a lubricator of the brain. Perhaps the attraction is that, whereas in primitive societies sexual dressing up was obligatory, in our open society it is a question of choice. Nevertheless, the atavism remains. Our ancestors needed the fig leaf; we may need other adornment – to get a laugh.

GASPS

Rubber

RUBBER ENTHUSIASTS form a numerous fraternity throughout the world, though the only common feature they share is having fun with rubber. They wear garments of latex, or like making love on latex, or being made love to by partners wearing latex.

The appeal is partially tactile, partially the sense of heat and sweatiness, partially the very good reason that these garments can be washed absolutely clean. (Salt water, the manufacturers warn, is not good for latex.)

You can now get custom tailored sex fun clothes of latex, tropique rubber, reina rubber, rubber backed satin, even rubber backed nylon. The colours are sophisticated, there being black, blue, mauve, plum red, green, yellow, and white to name a few. All the varieties of rubber also come in semi-transparent finish.

For women: long dresses, mini skirts, pyjamas, nighties. 'Alluring figure-hugging suit' (looks like a diving suit) with 'main zip at back or front and through the crotch'. Rubber bras and panties in many designs, including pantaloons and bloomers. Full length stockings and dresses with aprons.

For men: snugly fitted divers' headgear, giving a smooth profile to the pate, briefs, pyjamas, dressing gowns, T-shirts. In general the men's range is not as wide as the women's.

The more bizarre outfits include male briefs with built in sheath and women's suits with latex insertions for the vagina.

Leather

ENTHUSIASTS OF the treated hides of animals are even more numerous than rubber fans. Leather is more available than rubber, so more clothes can be bought as everyday wear and then passed into sexual service when required. There are leather briefs for men and women, leather bikinis, long thigh boots, masks, belts, cloaks, coats and more.

The drawback about a penchant for leather is that it can be very expensive. The real enthusiasts find the money well spent, since they use these garments as props in their love-making scenarios with the careful budgeting of a BBC-TV producer watching his set costs. But for most of us to shell out fivers for an exotic pair of boots or a corset of 1000 laces, we want more than a single titillation, and often these garments lack the charm to cause us to use them again.

Hiring such wear is a prudent first step for those of you who have not ventured into the tactile treats of leather. You may find you are turned on in a manner worth taking an overdraft for, but otherwise you will be glad to be able to send the sex props back.

Deviations

OH DEAR, everyone is a deviant, so there is little point in trying to define one. There is a great deal of point, however, in making clear which avenues of deviation are worth exploring and which are blind alleys with precipices at the end.

Some men like the feel of rubber, and so do some women. If they dress up in the stuff, and play about according to taste, and make love, all well and good. But if someone has to go it alone while dressed in a rubber replica of Mickey Mouse, then clearly his or her partner is not going to get much fun (nor are they in the long run).

Any sexual activity entered into freely and without duress, which causes no damage to the body or the sense of worth of either partner, and which leads to full genital intercourse most of the time, is acceptable. It may be worth trying what John and Jane get something out of, even if it seems strange.

Mutual masturbation

BRINGING ONESELF to a climax is practised by most men and women, even when happily married. Orgasms are intense and acute but the danger is that couples who value their companionship may be wasting the seed of greater things. We found that well adjusted couples masturbated a lot, but often did so together.

The man can soon learn to please his partner with fingers, massaging the labia and clitoris, just as the woman can stimulate the penis manually. For both sexes there is a sense of luxury – and providing both have learned their art – a welcome relaxation in being masturbated to a climax. The woman, in particular, can enjoy the delicious assurance of knowing she will be stimulated until she reaches full orgasm. The man, too, has the pleasure of orgasm without the strenuous exercise of his thighs and back. Cosy, caring, and companionable. Thoroughly recommended.

In many cases, the couples end the mutual caring session with intromission so that the ejaculation is done in the vagina. There is a variant, other than 69, which is rewarding enough to be mentioned. Here the penis itself is used as a finger to massage the lips and the clitoris. Either the man or the woman can so manipulate it. In doing this, he is masturbating at the same time so that it will probably produce quick orgasm in himself and his partner. The same applies if the woman is using the penis head to masturbate herself and him at the same time.

The rewards are enormous for this tiny expenditure of energy. But some care in preparative learning is needed, since clumsiness can result in an abraded glans or a bruised clitoris. Couples can practise with different positions, while the use of lubricants is also useful.

Bondage

BEING TIED up means your partner can do anything they like to you – so watch out for surprises! To most healthy psyches, the sensation of being utterly helpless is only acceptable in the presence and at the mercy of a trusted loved one. Bondage then, can nurture trust. But there are obvious safety rules. Don't tie anything around the neck, never use a gag, and never leave the bound person alone, especially if they are face down.

Fans of bondage have said they prefer to use scarves rather than ropes or chains, these latter being too full of unpleasant connotations in our often violent world. Being tied to a bed in an X position gives extensive possibilities for love bites on bottoms or nibbles on navels, depending on whether you are facing up or down. For some extraordinary reason, men often experience a rush of sexual desire on finding their familiar partner so unfamiliarly arranged. Women having their men in the X position report remarkable boosts to the imagination. Slow tickling of genitals is a favourite ploy.

Besides the X position, try tying the feet only or the arms only. Bondage is worth exploring, even if only to exercise muscles that haven't had a work out in years, but it should never go to extremes.

Slaps and Corporal punishment

TAKE YOUR partner over your lap and smack their buttocks. Do it vigorously. Men get erections when this is done to them, and also when they do it. Women lubricate extremely quickly, either as the passive or dominant partner.

Other forms of corporal punishment need to be approached with caution. Slaps on the bum, however, really can be recommended. The mixture of shock and contact is a decided turn on, merely vigorous horseplay.

Humiliation

IF YOUR relationship is very role stereotyped, with the man being the bread earner and the woman at home, and with associated dominance in the male – we do not say this is a consequence, but merely identify the roles opted for by many couples – then male humiliation games work well for sexual fun.

The man takes all his clothes off and has a lead put around his wrist. He is then made to walk around the house on all fours with his lady tugging on the lead. She asserts he will soon be led to a pre-arranged place of lovemaking, and warns him to perform with gusto or be smacked on his buttocks. Indeed, the smacking can be done anyway, insinuating that he needs correction for his abysmal personal habits – they may be reiterated to increase his shame.

When signs of extreme sexual agitation are noticed, usually a huge and throbbing erection, the moment of coupling can be chosen – by the woman of course.

Interest can be added by dressing up. Both partners can invest in all manner of kinky gear, though surprisingly, a chaste housecoat works wonders too. Why these simple games result in remarkable erections and vulval wetness is open to analysis. In Freudian terms, one can say that the man voluntarily surrenders his ego and id, thereby allowing his animal libido full rein. In relationships where the woman dominates, this game is reversed and she becomes the subject of humiliation. Both partners can experience the excitement of taking on new dimensions of personality, a curiously enriching and enlivening feeling. If couples cannot do this, it may suggest that their roles are becoming too set, their lifestyles too rigid, even that what was once a role has become a fixed trait of character. In healthy sex there are no fixed rules. Both partners should be expressive in varying things.

Arab straps, love-balls and enlargers

YOU DON'T need to put dangerous harnesses on your scrotum and penis, nor sheath yourself with rings of metal which create small electric currents, nor yet again insert your poor phallus into a suction device in hopes to make it bigger – you don't if you are looking for sex fun. Sex fun means, among other things, lack of anxiety, so you can't have much fun if you are anxious. Sex is about bodily and personal nakedness. Men who actually like women, and love one, are seldom impotent. When they are, the cause is not usually of a sexual nature, but because of a general run down of the whole system – for instance, from too much worry about work. Similarly, incapacity in women who like men, and love one, arises from systemic causes, not sexual ones.

We found no male who was having a full sexual life using

enlargers, and their penis size when erect ranged from very small (10 centimetres) to large (23 centimetres and above). The insertion of rubber or hard balls into the vagina so that sexual stimulation occurs as a woman walks is in the same anxious category as the male counterparts. Again, we found no women having full sexual lives using these devices. Good natured friends have bought partners such things, mostly as a giggle.

Clitoral and vaginal stimulators

THIS EXTRAORDINARILY rich range of aids, according to the reports we received, really do work for some people.

Basically the clitoral stimulators are various devices worn around the base of the erect phallus. At the point of utmost thrust, these devices come into contact with the clitoris. Since many men still have a hazy idea about this little organ – and miss it going in and coming out – the use of a clitoral stimulator can bring great delight to the erstwhile starved partner.

There are many different kinds. The most basic is a ring of rubber, plastic or leather with a feather, rubber tongue or some such protuberance. It is worn on the upper side of the penis shaft at the bottom. The names of the device are remarkable: Jewel of India, Man O' War, give some idea of the exotic associations made. Some are worn half-way up the penile shaft, and these not only tickle the clitoris and the lips as the penis thrusts in and out, but stimulate the walls of her vagina too. Well worth experimenting with to find one that suits; their price is such that a handy supply can be built up.

A little care needs to be taken when first using these objects, since they can lacerate and bruise. But once mastered it's good fun for her and for him, specially because he knows he's doing better than usual.

Couples rarely used them habitually, but rather in the spirit of this book, as a bit of fun on festive nights. Recommended by many of our reporters.

Other stimulators to be worn on the erect phallus are exotic condoms with bumps, protuberances and rubbery gills, all of which add variation. You can now get contraceptive sheaths in pink, black or gold, with or without embellishments. Some women shop around to find the most exciting assortment, and then play 'dress the pussy cat', trying first this one and that on her lover's erect phallus, until her fancy is suited.

Condoms, plain or fancy, are a fine fun aid in anal sex. After the desired fun has been had there, the penis is withdrawn and the sheath discreetly discarded, leaving an entirely fresh phallus for oral and vaginal duets. It really is quite amazing that so many handbooks on sex ignore both the aesthetic and hygienic rules of anal sex. The sheath provides a superb aid here.

Finally, there are various finger stalls available. These had next to no devotees among active lovers of long intimacy, who prefer naked fingers.

Performance creams and pills

NONE OF the couples reporting to us used any artificial aid to potency or libido. Since no one knows the seminal basis of female urgency or male ability, it is hardly plausible that cheaply produced, expensively wrapped pills and lotions are going to work.

However, there is a certain arcane fascination about these apothecary products. You can buy Red Stallion or Black Tiger capsules which promise rather frightening potency. The advertising copy cites, 'Iron hooves pounding the rugged turf'. Fans of zoo sex TV programmes might find them amusing, but as an authentic aid to sex fun, such pills are at best a placebo.

Stamina lotions are used to deaden the sensation of the penis glans so that ejaculation does not come quickly. They contain a variety of local anaesthetics. Clearly not to be recommended, since erection for a long period is a learned response, entirely under conscious control. We found none of our couples using these chemicals. It might be fun once or twice – if you like having intercourse in the same way that you have a tooth filled after an injection: you know something is going on, but you can't feel it.

Sex Books and magazines

BOOKS ON sex are a delicate area. There are so many of them and few stand the test of time. Above all, people run the danger of being passive victims to a point of view, which is far too often moralistic or mechanistic, and misleading. No book list can satisfy all predilictions. However, some books do have a vein of sexual truth in them well worth mining from the seams of lesser value.

The *Karma Sutra* is a delight of Eastern eroticism, a little biased in favour of the male but containing much rich evocation. There is a delightful passage on the belly and the waist. *Joy of Sex,* by Alex Comfort, has many good ideas.

Few others seem worth mentioning. The spate of sex manuals usually suffer from a mechanical humourless approach. Simply do not buy a sex book on mail order unless it is returnable. They have a habit of being all good title, good cover, and pap inside.

Many couples use magazines as a sex aid, since looking at pretty women is not entirely a male preserve of pleasure. The form was to browse in bed with a magazine, and to discuss various assets of the models. Whereas male pin-ups have restricted currency among women, and are effectively bankrupt with heterosexual men, sexy women seem to be welcomed by both heterosexual partners. Clearly there is scope here for a serious research programme, but as a sex fun aid, pin-ups are a possibility.

Some care is required in picking the magazine. The ones we found used often were soft core porn or glamour magazines. The general opinion among our couples is that there is no fun in hard core porn – no mystery and certainly no eroticism. The more telling point is that hard core porn magazines have no affection in them, and this is offputting to couples playing the game of love.

Soft core means that erect penises are not shown. I found few fans among our couples for hard porn.

Interestingly, one couple reported the wife's love of magazines about model train systems, and another said she enjoyed reading Popular Mechanic with her husband.

Vibrators

THESE ARE electrical and usually in the shape of a penis; they vibrate with sufficient energy to impart a warm tingle at the point of contact. Usually sold as a solo sex aid, these articles are useful adjuncts for couples, and it is surprising that the manufacturers seem unaware that so many couples use them.

Vibrators come in many variations. The common presumption by retailers in their catalogues is that they will all be used by someone called a 'liberated woman', on herself. This belies the huge repertoire of games we have found couples playing with these devices.

Because of its shape, the vibrator can be inserted into the vagina, anus or mouth – but it can also be held against the penis, between the breasts, under the armpit, against nipples, inside the thighs, on the palms of the hands, on the buttock and facial cheeks, on lips, ear-lobes – in fact, anywhere upon the skin.

It is essential to buy a well designed vibrator that can be easily cleaned. Don't get one that plugs into mains. There is always some danger of electrical leakage, which is unimportant if the vibrator has its own battery supply. The minor shock that a short circuit from batteries can give may be a bonus, but the discharge from the mains is more than any AC or DC couple can bear.

When buying a vibrator, rub your fingers over the whole surface. Many cheaper models have bad fitting joints which feel rough or sharp to the touch. We have had many reports of hapless persons being nicked in the tenderest of places and at the most awkward of moments by these imperfections. It must be totally acceptable to the fingers to be acceptable as a sex aid.

Regarding texture, personal preference is the guide. You can get vibrators with little rubber points, with a casing of gold or silver plastic, in rubber or latex. Some are fixed in shape, others can be bent in any position. You can get vibrators especially designed to be put into your mouth.

We found that most lovers have a spate of vibration exploration, and then forget all about the device. Nevertheless, the price of a cheaper vibrator is well worth the half dozen times you may use it on one another.

The idea of the vibrator can tickle most people's fancy as well as their body. Your lover knows all your sensitive spots, so it's rather titillating to wonder where are you going to get vibrated next. Naturally, you slip into your customary love-making at the end of a session.

Another vibrator game is to insert it in the anus. Women find it fun to feel the familiar, loving penis in the vagina while being vibrated at the back. Men are driven to greater heights of thrust with a vibrator in their anus. Part of the fun comes from the transmitted vibrations – if your man has a vibrator in his rear end and is entering you, you can feel it. Similarly, vibrators in the woman's anus can be felt in the vagina by the male's penis.

It is, of course, impossible to take these devices seriously. Even the ones that are worn on the penis during intercourse are nothing more than a point of departure. We found no couples who use them habitually – but they can be fun for a few times.

Dildoes

DILDOES ARE shaped to resemble the erect penis anatomically. Some even have retractable foreskins. Usually made of moulded rubber or latex, they can be purchased with or without vibrators, with or without devices to simulate ejaculation. In general, we found active lovers rarely use these devices, but there are some ploys with sufficient frisson to be worth including in a repertoire.

Some women find it exciting to strap on a dildo, usually of outrageous colouration, and penetrate their men anally. The experience for a heterosexual male borders on rape – not a pleasant sensation – while latent homosexuals may discover their preference for this kind of lovemaking. So as a sex fun gambit, dildo strappings clearly can lead to undesirable results.

We found that some lovers use dildoes during normal intercourse, as anal stimulators, or for stroking each other. Sometimes oral stimulation with a dildo is used.

In general, in active lovers the dildo is rarely encountered. Curiously, the notion that it is 'unfair to the penis' to even think of using a dildo cropped up several times. We found that the penis, like the vulva, is often thought of as a friend to the feast, and not as a mere organ.

RESOURCES

Personality

I HAVE used a clear and flexible classification of sexual personality for many years in research on marriage stability. In this scheme, *Ectosexuals* are people whose sexual responses and needs are on the surface of the body. For example, they have unusually sensitive nipples, genitalia, and mouths. The skin itself is sensitive all over the body. *Endosexuals*, in contrast have deeper responses. Their tongues, vaginal walls, rectal walls, and deeper tissues are more sensitive than the outside of their bodies. *Extrosexuals* respond sexually with their muscles, whether penis, vagina, or the whole force of the physique. These are clear-cut examples of three clear-cut sexual personalities. They are extremes.

Accordingly, we would expect that most people have a mixture of these traits in varying proportions. Indeed, surveys show this to be the case, and most people score average values in all three of the following questionnaires dealing with sexual personality. It is very useful to determine your own rating so you can then explore sexuality with a new insight. Try these tests.

Ectosexual personality

The Ectosexual is capable of great passion, but only in a supportive, emotionally secure, relationship. Hence ectosexuals favour marriage and the domestic scene. In the male there is the tendency to be over-sensitive to the emotional climate, so that erection difficulties can occur rather frequently if he feels unloved. In the female, a fear of being penetrated is common, especially with inept lovers. Key sex fun requirements for both are gentleness, caring support, a stable domestic life, and above all, peace and quiet to enable them to enjoy their sexuality.

Test:

1 Are your movements tense and restrained?
2 Do you react quickly, perhaps too quickly, to changes of temperature?
3 Do you prefer to be alone or with one or two close friends rather than in a crowd?
4 Do you keep your feelings to yourself rather than confide in others?
5 Do you avoid crowds and parties?
6 Do you find it difficult to keep to a routine?
7 Is your voice quiet?
8 Are you unusually sensitive to pain?
9 Is your sleep disturbed?
10 When you are upset, do you prefer to be alone?

Scores: 1 for yes, 0 for no.
7+ predominantly ectosexual.
4-6 average.
3— insignificant ectosexuality.

Endosexual personality

Comfort, courtesy, style: these are the cravings and the needs of Endosexuals. Both men and women have to be, love to be, cossetted, and this implies a tendency to be passive. They relish sexual enjoyment, but the less effort they have to make to get it, the more they like it.

Test:

1 Do you tend to move and stand in a relaxed way?
2 Is physical comfort a major part of your life.
3 Do you get great pleasure in eating?
4 Do you like to eat with other people?
5 Are you a stickler for etiquette?
6 Do you have a large number of acquaintances, all of whom you like, but in rather a superficial manner?
7 Do you sleep deeply and well?
8 Do you find that food and/or alcohol relaxes you?
9 When upset do you seek out other people rather than hide away?
10 Are your family relationships important to you?

Scores: 1 for yes, 0 for no.
7+ predominantly endosexual.
4-6 average.
3— insignificant endosexuality.

Extrosexual personality

The Extrosexual is the sexual stormtrooper, whether male or female. They relish sexual aggression, and they are the aggressors. Male extrosexuals prefer highly penetrable positions in their female partners, are avid for anal intercourse, and often too enthusiastic for fellatio, in which they often thrust too energetically. Indeed, these men like to ring the changes on the three orifices, and are not above moving the woman about like a doll. Female extrosexuals use their tongues, nipples, clitoris, hands, and even toes in an aggressive, penetrating way on the male orifices and surface.

When these women practise fellatio, only a fool would think he was dominant. They take over, devour, invade men's bodies. Both sexes are able to have sex without moral agonising, at the drop of a hint. Intercourse is usually intense, fast, and acute, with quick orgasms. But they make up for the lack of longevity by frequency. It is very common, especially when young, for extrosexuals to have intercourse several times a day.

Test:

1 Are you assertive in your movements?
2 Do you enjoy adventurous sports such as mountaineering, driving, water skiing?
3 Do you dominate others, or at least try to?
4 Do you have a no-nonsense, direct manner?
5 Is it difficult to intimidate you physically?
6 Do you revel in competition?
7 Have several people said you are ruthless?
8 Is your voice effortlessly loud, even when you are not trying to make yourself heard?
9 Can you stand pain easily?
10 When you are upset, do you seek relief in physical action?

Scores: 1 for yes, 0 for no.
7+ predominantly extrosexual.
4-6 average
3— insignificant extrosexuality.

Implications of the scores Your sexual profile is given by the mixture of traits. Most people will score a profile of 5-5-5, and the vast majority of people will lie between 4-4-4 and 6-6-6.

The possibilities for sex fun on determining your sexual personality are restricted only by your imagination. For example, if you are an Extrosexual male who scored 2-2-8, and your partner is an Endosexual who scored 2-8-2, why not try being your lady's passive victim? Similarly, the extrosexual female with the ectosexual male can pretend to be passive, and he physically dominant.

However, we must remember that personality changes and so, therefore, does behaviour. It is neglect of this principle that so often leads to stereotyping – and so to boredom. Habit is part of sexual fulfilment, coming after the first novel rush. But habit must give way to new activities if sex is to be fun. For this reason, an insight into sexual personality provides ideas for new departures.

Here, then are some hints for enlarging your repertoire of sexual activities, according to personality.

To please the

Endosexual woman—	buy the best wine you can and cuddle her while she drinks it; invest in silk sheets and chintz curtains.
Ectosexual woman—	read Proust or Erica Jong to her kissing her between pages; put on a cassette or record of Chopin piano pieces during foreplay.
Extrosexual woman—	give her her head and learn to be passive; turn up in chains or strait jacket.

To please the

Endosexual man—	home cooking and a bottle of wine will make him delirious, especially if you pat his bottom and kiss him gently.
Ectosexual man—	talk to him about his hobby as you make love even if his hobby is – as it is likely to be – calculus, Mayan archaeology, or Dryden's political pamphlets; remember also that all ectosexuals love perfumes.
Extrosexual man—	be the incarnation of a sex object;

everybody is a sex object to somebody
some of the time.

These insights need developing. You get a good start if you bear in mind that most slim people have a large component of ectosexuality, most muscular people a large measure of extro-sexuality, and most plump or fat people a large element of endosexuality (see Physique).

Sexual approach

EXTROSEXUALS ARE characterised by dominance, energy, and no-nonsense lack of sentimentality. They don't indulge in much foreplay, or care about introduction. The male is the 'stud' of popular folklore; the female is the aggressor, using men as sex objects – mere appendages to a penis which they gobble with mouth, vulva or vagina.

A female Ectosexual will prefer cunnilingus to vaginal penetration, nipple kissing rather than nipple sucking. The male Ectosexual prefers to massage the clitoris with tongue or glans rather than penetrating his partner. Endosexuals prefer deep massage to stroking and like to lie and be taken.

Partners with one predominantly extrosexual and the other largely Endosexual find themselves in trouble: one is too forceful and the other too passive. In this circumstance, much opportunity is lost for fun, lost indeed for personal growth. Accordingly, it is a good thing to pretend that you are rampantly ectosexual or extrosexual, or whatever is unlike your usual approach. It should not be long before boredom is a thing of the past (see Personality).

Sexual stereotypes are the bane of sex fun, the put downer of personality, the frost rather than the icing on the cake of sexual enjoyment. If you are locked into one of these stereotypes, your sexuality is impoverished because of the restricted role you play. However, if you become aware of the sexual repertoire of sexual stereotypes, they can then become new methods for you to try.

An obvious stereotype is the excessively macho male, bulging jock strap, rippling muscles, rough manner and constantly randy. One female stereotype is the submissive sex slave, a door mat there to enact her master's whims.

A woman can be as 'macho' as the male stereotype, and a man as slavish as the female stereotype.

Sex fun is richer when you modify the stereotypical behaviour whatever your sex. Remember, the stereotyping of men as aggressive and women as passive sexually has a wider implication in the social context. So avoid stereotyping.

Physique

CLEARLY, SOME matings have in-built strengths, others in-built weaknesses. This would be reason enough to consider your partner from the point of view of physique, but identification of physique is fun in itself.

Height and weight are an approximate guide to physique, though overweight can mislead. The table below can serve to distinguish the slim builds from the heavy builds.

Height in inches	Weight in pounds			
	slim builds		heavy builds	
	men	women	men	women
61	84	90	140	124
63	93	99	150	136
66	107	114	160	156
69	122	130	182	176
72	139	148	206	199
75	157	—	230	—

Sex fun is all about giving your beloved as much of you as often and as fully as possible. You stand a better chance of doing that well if you know the potential of your own body and of your partner's. The table below shows how body build has contributed to stable marriage. It tells you enough to be a guide to using sexual skills better.*

Build of partners	Marriages breaking up before seven years %
Both partners very slim	10
Slim man, average woman	12½
Slim man, large-built woman	7
Both partners average	15
Average man, slim woman	16
Average man, large-built woman	13
Both partners heavy-built	7
Slim woman, heavy-built man	40
Average woman, heavy-built man	8

Now work through the following routine, both of you in the nude. Be scientific about this: use a notebook and observe the variations of skin texture, the muscle tone, the set of bones, and the sweep of the torso. The individual case, as the author Somerset Maugham discovered when a medical student, always departs from the text book 'normal'. Use your fingers to determine texture, and sweep the eye up from toe to crown and down again, observing from front, back,

* For more details, see my *Love Bodies* (Arrow 1982).

and side. Observe also in lying, standing, kneeling and stretching positions.

Features	Slim types	Large build types
skin	tans with difficulty; inconspicuous pores; feels thin when you pinch it	tans easily; large pores; feels springy when you pinch it
muscles	long and stringy to touch	full; feels round and like hard rubber (even on a woman of this type)
joints (ankles, knees, elbows)	surface of bones is ridged, sharp	bone surface smooth and rounded
face	delicate; chiselled; aquiline	rugged; strongly made
neck	thin	muscular, tendons thick
ribs	visible, thin, easily pressed in (careful!)	feel like barrel staves, difficult to press in.

Average builds have characteristics formed from a blend of the opposite traits here. For example, their muscles are not particularly stringy nor full and hard, but are quite strong and evident. Slim people are seldom extrosexuals, who are usually of a rugged physique.

Only a minority of people will fall exclusively into one column or the other, but the tendency will be obvious.

Understanding the physique can bring illuminations for giving and taking sexual pleasure.

Gentleness

AS THE years pass, so may familiarity increase while tenderness runs the risk of decreasing. Wise couples have ritualised their gentleness to one another in soft, kind words, even at breakfast, in polite discretion, and in a caring disposition. Needless to say, this reaps infinite rewards in sex fun, for the persistent application of gentleness creates a substratum upon which loving erections can be built, and rivers of reciprocal lubricity can flow.

Sex fun implies gentleness, which must be regarded as an essential, irreplaceable ingredient of a lasting relationship. Paradoxically, by treating one another during the daily round with the courtesy we reserve for strangers, greater intimacies result. Flowers, chocolate, cups of tea, a bottle of scotch, little presents regularly, smiles, endearments, kisses, embraces, and cuddling – all create the atmosphere in which the libido can flourish. Gentleness is strongly recommended to all couples at whatever stage of development.

Menstruation

MANY OF our active couples make love during menstruation. Indeed, many women have heightened sexual needs during menstruation, and feel a special togetherness during menstrual intercourse. There are no health dangers, but the aesthetics of a bloody bed are dubious. Rubber sheeting is not to everyone's taste, but it is practical. In any event, it is the gentlemanly thing to do to remove the soiled bedclothes after the fun, and to tuck your partner up.

Part of the appeal of sex during menstruation is that the flow of blood can induce feelings of the loss of virginity: both partners triumphant in that first lovemaking. If you did, in fact, begin sexual life together, the symbolic monthly re-enactment of the breaking of the hymen can be one of your marriage's specially nostalgic acts.

A bonus is that having sex during menstruation often relieves women of menstrual cramps.

The menstrual flow is heady, but often has a singularly sweet aroma. Though it differs from woman to woman, the odour is often reminiscent of new mown hay or a rich red wine (Bordeaux, I've noticed).

A practical point: if you use tampons, it is wise to take a douche prior to intercourse, because tampons block the flow of blood and cause some clotting. This can be an irritant to you and him if not eliminated beforehand.

Semen

ALTHOUGH THOUGHT to be white, the colour is slightly yellow to green in a healthy man. This is because semen contains traces of riboflavin, a B vitamin which also gives the yellowish cast to milk.

Sexually active men should be aware that in each ejaculation they lose many nutrients because semen is highly nutritive. It contains substantial amounts of vitamins and some trace metals, notably zinc and nickel, which are found in meat and the germs of seeds. Other trace minerals in semen are also found in yeast and black molasses.

To ensure that your blood levels of nutrients remain high, you should eat black molasses from time to time (it makes quite a nice drink with hot milk and brown sugar). Brewers yeast can be added to gravies and sauces for a nutritional boost.

An active, highly mobile batch of sperms in the ejaculation is also dependent on nutrition. Many women report pleasure in feeling the movement of the ascending sperms – but there must be many active sperm; you can't feel one. Sex fun fans should therefore keep in training so their sperms will be too.

Contraception

THE SENSE of freedom that good contraception gives is essential for sex fun. The various methods vary not only in efficiency, but also in aesthetics, satisfaction, and fun. The next eight sections deal with contraceptive methods.

Sheaths

The efficacy of sheaths can be shown by statistics of the number of pregnancies per 100 married and unmarried women per 12 months. Most surveys give the 'French letter' a rating of one pregnancy per 100 women per year. An average level of intercourse frequency in the age range 18-39 is 200 per woman per year, so the sheath is an excellent preventive method. Indeed, the failure rate can be attributed largely to misuse.

But there are inherent dangers. The sheath can only be put on an erect penis, and by that time secretions have already begun to flow, so these early emissions contain mobile sperms. Then, when intercourse is completed, the phallus shrinks. This often leaves the condom within the vagina, and the sperms can escape from the open end to begin their long swim up the vaginal canal. The obvious lesson is that you put it on with care, and you take it out immediately after coitus. Unsheathing is also fraught, however, because the ejaculation inside the sheath can be spilled. Some pregnancies also result from re-insertion of the unsheathed penis, which is still alive with active spermatozoa.

Sheaths deaden sensitivity – like having a bath with a wet suit on – but many couples don't seem to mind this. Probably more undesirable is the lack of the thrill for women of feeling the force and the heat of the ejaculation. Many women resent this impoverishment, and also miss the quiet content obtained by feeling – they report it – the movement of the sperms.

It is essential to ensure that the sheath meets at least minimal safety specifications. In the UK, you should use only those condoms given the British Standards Kite Mark. The fun sheaths discussed earlier *are not contraceptives.*

Turn the ensheathing into a ritual to avoid awkward breaks in the tempo of sex: when the penis is erect, the woman kisses and fondles it as she puts the condom on. Some couples have created interesting gambits of unsheathing. As soon as the ejaculation is over, or as soon as the phallus begins to shrink, the woman holds the penis at its shaft end to prevent the sheath from slipping off, and he withdraws. He then lies on his back and she 'disrobes' the phallus, making sure the sheath is put firmly aside. With oral stimulation, a new erection can be coaxed – and a new sheath applied.

There are a sufficient number of people interested in latex to find exploration of these rituals rewarding. The bonus is that he keeps his hands away from the spermatozoa, and she controls the sheathing and unsheathing so that it is safer. A must for women with maladroit lovers.

Diaphragms and caps

THESE ARE rubber discs which are inserted to cover the top of the cervix. They are about one third as safe as sheaths, but their efficacy is increased by using a spermicide with them. Family planning clinics or your doctor can show you how to put them in correctly. If the partner learns how to do it, it might prove to be a turn-on for you both.

These caps are often worn for some hours, but they must be taken out and washed regularly. They are not good for deep-penetration positions because the penis bangs up against them. They are, however, excellent for the missionary position, when their presence is not felt. This can lead to more careful attention to lips and clitoris than otherwise may be paid.

Rather more rewarding than sheaths in that they do not cut down the glans-vagina contact, they are not quite so reliable. But even at two pregnancies per 100 women per year, they can be regarded as eminently practicable and relatively safe.

The Pill

HERE FULL freedom of intercourse is assured, though the failure rate is about the same as for diaphragms. The problem is that up to 25 per cent of women using the pill face a health hazard. However, the risk is about the same as that accompanying pregnancy, so you have to weigh the costs yourselves. The pill renders the uterus wall inhospitable to the fertilised egg through hormonal imbalance, so it is important to get the right mix of hormones. This can only be done by trial and error, under your doctor's care, to find one which suits. The vast majority of younger women, say under 30, have little difficulty, but there is one school of medical opinion which is suspicious of bringing about the cessation of menstruation (the effective action of the pill) in young women. I would go along with that. It seems biologically unwise for young women not to menstruate for the best part of a decade.

Obviously there is no clear-cut path here, but the paths are nonetheless reasonably signposted. When you are very young, sheaths and caps, although not as safe as the pill, have no health risks. If you have had your family by your early twenties, however, it is not unreasonable to advise the use of the correct contraceptive pill until your early thirties.

Coils

THE INTERESTING thing about coils (and the pill) is that fertilisation can actually take place – that is, the sperm can meet an egg and penetrate it. But the coil irritates the wall of the uterus to the extent of rendering implantation by the egg unlikely.

The failure rate of the coil is rather higher than the pill, on about the same level as caps. There is also an attendant health risk, affecting about 2 per cent of women. Bleeding, infection and even outside-the-womb pregnancies have been reported, so full consultation with your doctor is essential. So is monitoring by periodic checks when you are wearing one. The vast majority of women suffer no ill effects.

The coil does not interfere with glans-vagina contact, but some women experience a tenderness on deep penetration, which they had not done before. There is also a problem with the tiny string which hangs down the vaginal canal from the coil. Very sensitive penis heads feel it as a persistent scratch.

The coil is most widely used by women after having a child, and frequently proves best in the over-thirties.

Pessaries

THESE FOAMING materials are injected into the vagina.

Comic or off-putting, as you see it, they do not have a good success rate. Some men feel like they are dipping their penis into a frothing shaving bowl. Often used in conjunction with caps. We know of no couple who stuck with this method for long.

Holding back and withdrawal

THESE ARE disastrous methods, both in terms of failure and in terms of turning fun into anxiety. In holding back, the woman is left waiting and the man goes away still tense. There are possibilities of using this technique to prolong love play and to build up higher and higher tensions to a thunderous climax. But as a contraceptive method, it is extremely poor. The same goes for withdrawal just before ejaculation. Messy, unaesthetic, and, because sperms have been moving out of the penis and up the vagina long before ejaculation, a poor contraceptive method.

First aid

VIGOROUS COUPLES are bound to make love at some time or other without precautions. So what to do? As soon as possible after coitus, sit on the bed, open your legs, bend your head between them and cough. This sets up reverberations along the vagina, shaking the semen down. Then go into the bathroom and wash in the bidet, or if you haven't got one, douche in the bath.

Another technique of self-help is to put half a lemon up the vagina after squeezing it free of juice and washing it under warm water. This acts like a cap, and the remnant of juice is spermicidal. Variants of this method are well known in many cultures. Half of a rubber ball was used in Italy during Mussolini's regime, for example, when contraceptives were banned. Vinegar is a spermicide too.

Sterilisation

A DRASTIC surgical solution that is irreversible. In women,

the operation severs the tubes leading from the ovaries to the uterus, so that eggs cannot descend and be fertilised. A simple procedure, but not without risks. In men, the sperm duct is severed. Psychologically, there are important factors to be considered. Women report that they feel that some of a man's attractiveness is lost when he is sterilised. Words like castration and eunuch pepper their completed questionnaires. In view of the excellent battery of contraception methods which leave the option for pregnancy open, sterilisation has little to recommend it except in exceptional circumstances.

Rhythm method

UNFORTUNATELY, THIS method is usually a conception instead of a contraception, since the usual side product is a pregnancy. The method is based on the fact that, while the ovum is still in the ovary or when it has passed out of the uterus, the woman is infertile. The time to avoid intercourse is during the period when peak fertility occurs – namely, when the ovum is in the uterus. This time is very imprecise because it cannot be known if the ovum will stay there one day or five days. Furthermore, it is very difficult to say when the egg is actually there.

Ovulation occurs about half-way through the menstrual cycle and can be determined by keeping track of temperatures orally until the peak temperature is reached, which is the sign that ovulation has taken place. You will not get much joy playing about with thermometers in the anus, which is how temperature can be measured in this case. Men should try it on themselves just to see how women feel. In any case, a peak of temperature may be nothing more than an incipient cold, so there is no guarantee that ovulation has been determined. Furthermore, thermometers can be dangerous when inserted by untrained people.

The one slight advantage of the rhythm method is that it can give you both a chance to mime doctor and patient or teacher and student in sex fun play. You do this by examining the fluids in the vagina to try to find the ovum that has passed down. However, having been a biochemistry teacher for many years, and having observed that most students – even though equipped with high-power microscopes and three A levels – still manage to confuse sperms with glucose crystals, it would be imprudent of me to suggest more than that there is a very minor chance of your catching the tiny egg in its descent. If by chance you do, then you can be sure of having infertile intercourse for about 20 days afterwards – unless your partner happens to pass another egg a few hours later, as sometimes occurs. Then you will have had your fun just as she is at her most fertile. Indeed, if you want to get pregnant by design and not accident, you can use the rhythm method to time your coitus at the point of greatest fertility.

Clearly, there is much beauty in the rhythm method, but the bald facts are it doesn't work for the majority of people for long. Sooner or later you will have a fertile union.

Proception

IT IS CURIOUS that contraception is a word known by everyone, but proception is unfamiliar to most. Yet many couples strive for years to achieve fertile intercourse. Impediments to fertilisation of a medical nature are beyond the scope of this book, but to have intercourse with one's beloved in order to make a child takes sex fun into joy and joy into ecstasy.

It has been proved that if the scrotal sac is cooled by ice water, the mobility of the released sperm is enhanced. Indeed, the males of infertile couples were treated with ice bags, and fertility followed. Fun can be had if she massages his testicles with ice cubes or a cold compress. This bizarre – or delicious, according to taste – sex play increases the chance of fertilisation. Don't take this so far that chilling occurs, and never use ice cubes straight from the fridge; put them in water first.

Relaxed sex also appears to increase the chance of conception. This means using any or all of the techniques in this guide. Deep relaxation for deep penetration and reception is the aim. At full arousal, the chemical environment of the vagina is most hospitable to sperms, and aids their long trek up the canal into the uterus. Hence the importance of going deep before ejaculation. Indeed, with practise in the deep penetrant positions, the spermatozoa can be shot directly into the uterus. I am amazed to find that even sexually active couples seldom achieve such bliss. Yet, with gentle care – like the delicate finger of a gardener probing into a prize rose – the full flowering of the boudoir bouquet can be obtained.

Pregnancy

A TIME for very tender intercourse and gentle affection. During this period, you do not engage in athletic sex or anything smacking of the bizarre. Pregnancy is a time for enjoying the ultimate consummation of your love. When the baby has come, resumption of sex fun in gradually accelerating intensity over a period of a few months is the way to create new levels of mutual regard and happiness.

Fidelity

MUCH MALIGNED, little understood, faithfulness is the shield of sex fun. For one thing, fidelity is next to cleanliness. Armed with the knowledge that your partner and you have already exchanged all your body bacteria with no ill effects, and having no social diseases, you can explore the manifold possibilities of sexual intimacy without running the risk of catching the various venereal diseases, not to mention lice, fleas, fungi, and sexual herpes. VD has reached epidemic proportions. Promiscuity, then, is no longer fun – or rather, the profit and loss ledger now shows it to be on the debit side.

Faithful in body, trusting in mind, your nerves may without fear offer themselves up to raptures without doubt. No cause to wonder if you carry to the conjugal bed unwelcome reminders of extra-marital sex. No, the fragrance of faithfulness emanates from your every pore. Fidelity cements the foundation of your mutual sexuality, and towers of joy are erected.

So, in faith you can be both chaste and lascivious. Fidelity can support the fiercest passion and yet remain sweet, can sustain the doldrums to rise to new heights. Fidelity is the sweetest of love's bouquets: its fragrance, like its kisses, are a joy forever.

Infidelity

WHILE IT is true that unfaithfulness can excite nerves that other stimuli cannot reach, it has no recommendation whatsoever as a path to sex fun. We found no couple who felt it was worthwhile. Contrary to popular belief, swinging is a destroyer of sexual harmony, opening up rifts, not healing them. On the other hand, the isolated act of infidelity has caused many a spouse to hurry on home to the real, satisfying action. Threesomes and spouse swopping are not worth the effort, not least because of the danger of catching some noxious organism. For killing healthy belly laughs, there is nothing so sure as wondering if your partner is going to infect you.

He may be an Apollo and she a Venus de Milo, yet long

familiarity may have dulled their perception of each other's desirability. Try to see each other with other people's eyes and you might get as flirtatious as that interested party at your neighbour's the other night.

Fats

SMOOTH SKIN, sexuality, body contours, even your brain and nervous system depend on fat. How can that be true when all we hear about fat is that it is bad for you? The answer lies in discriminating between good and bad dietary fats. First, the basics.

Fat is the most concentrated form of energy. Most animal fats such as suet, lard and dripping contain a narrow spectrum of chemical types, mostly the ones you do not need. Pastries, gravies, hamburgers, then, are a bad dietary investment. You get huge amounts of calories for small amounts of vitamins and minerals.

In contrast, the fats you find in vegetable oils, nuts, the skins of fruits and vegetables, liver and fish, are very varied. The amount of fat is small, but of the highest quality. Cheese, butter, and to a lesser extent, yoghurt, also contribute to the wide mix of fats we must have.

Fats do not dissolve in water easily. That is why fat in your skin helps to prevent excessive drying. But the smooth quality of facial and body skin also depends on a substance found in association with stored fat. This is lecithin, which is found in concentrated form in liver, yolks of eggs and brains. They are used directly by the body to manufacture the smooth surface of skin cells.

Lecithins are used by cosmetic manufacturers for emollients – but it is far better to build from the inside, rather than rely on a cosmetic covering for the outside.

You have approximately 100,000,000,000,000 cells in your body and each one has a covering of skin called the lipid-protein membrane. The lipid refers to fat of the nature of lecithin. For each cell to function properly, it must have its lecithins. Body contours depend on this elastic membrane to retain their firm line.

The functioning of your brain also depends on fat. Like most living tissue, brain tissue is nearly three quarters water. Fat is the next most important constituent in the brain at 10 per cent, followed by protein at eight per cent. Each nerve fibre, on which you depend to send and receive messages from various parts of the body, is encased in a fatty sheath. This not only protects it, but actually takes part in the sending of nervous impulses.

A diet rich in animal fats tends to produce fat layers under the skin of a less fluid and less soft variety than those produced by foods giving mixed fats. It is a proven fact that the kind of fat you eat is reflected in the chemical composition under your skin. Indeed, an autopsy on your fat layer would give a very clear picture of the food you ate, easily distinguishing between fish eaters, red meat eaters, and total vegetarians.

Cellulite is a layer of rumpled fat. I have noticed it to be extremely common in people whose intake of animal fat is nearly half their calorie intake. In the cases where cellulite has been caught early enough, a smoother contour has resulted from rubbing olive oil into it. This use of olive oil is centuries old in Mediterranean countries.

Perhaps the most astonishing feature of our nervous system is that it appears to function continuously, although in fact there are minute gaps as an impulse moves along a nerve and jumps across a lacuna between it and the next nerve. This gap is called a synapse, and can only be bridged by a molecular jumper, which has the name of acetylcholine. Acetyl occurs in most fats. Choline is found only in specialised fats, being in rich supply in eggs, liver and, to a lesser extent, brains. They are clearly important to the nervous system.

So bad has the press been for fats that we often forget that four vitamins, A, D, E and K, are fatty in nature. Our preoccupation with cholesterol obscures the fact that we actually manufacture this substance ourselves. We need it, albeit in much smaller amounts than we eat it, to make a variety of important materials, not least of which are the sex hormones in both male and female sex organs.

Fats, then, must be eaten, but in a mix from the three main groups of plant and synthetic (unsaturated) varieties. A word of warning to those who live on an entirely cholesterol free diet, and who eat too much unsaturated fat without adding vitamin E: a Swedish colleague of mine who is a sex therapist has found among her patients a disproportionate number of impotent men whose diets are low in cholesterol and vitamin E. She is convinced that their diet and their impotence is related.

Energy

THE BASIC fuel for sex comes from food and is measured in calories. The diet should be watched by all sex fun fans in order to avoid obesity, which reduces sexual awareness and performance.

The amount of fuel we need can be seen from the table below, measured in calories required per 24 hours:

Women	Most life styles	Very active life style
18 +	2200	2600
Men		
18 +	2600	3300

Very active life styles include labouring and heavy

industrial work for men, and running a home with children and doing an active job for women.

Since sexual intercourse is equivalent to hard labour in energy consumption, one would hope that most readers of this book will graduate to the very active life style category.

Apply these rules:

1 Eat often and small – no heavy meals.

2 Eat breakfast – most overweight people feel too sick to eat breakfast.

3 Eat a varied diet – don't always have the same cereal, and try rice sometimes instead of potatoes.

4 Make sure you have every day:
Some vegetables
Some fruit
Some lean meat and/or fish
Some whole grains – brown rice, wholemeal bread
Some milk
Some cheese.

5 During the week have some beans and never miss green vegetables for more than one day.

6 An egg a week is good, two is better, one every day is bad.

7 Reduce the amount of solid fat you eat.

8 Eat liver once a fortnight.

9 Eat fresh rather than canned food.

10 Use honey rather than sugar – you can't eat so much honey.

11 Make up for menstrual blood loss by eating red meat for iron and drinking red wine.

Crying

WHEN TEARS flow after lovemaking, all is well. Crying not only cleanses the eyes, but releases residual tension. There is some evidence that the actual chemical products of stress are drained from the body through tears. So a bout of crying before, during, or after intercourse is an aid to sex fun.

But how do you cry? Watching weepy old movies is one way, and probably accounts for the huge following that late night TV has. Our couples often pet and cosset each other during the weepier moments, and that leads to lovemaking.

Men really interested in boosting their sex lives should steadfastly vow to weep at the first opportunity. Not only does this elicit deep raptures from your wife, but it also breaks down tension in your face, and further down the body. Tears are truly the waters of love.

Barter

WE STRIKE bargains in all walks of life, so why not in sexual life? The likelihood that the same thing will turn both partners on is small. But good natured lovers of long standing can soon agree to an exchange rate, the currency of which is up to the partners concerned.

For example, if one of your penchants is being spanked on the bottom with a velvet-gloved hand worn by your lover while she is attired in a raincoat and you are playing tapes of Wagner's *Siegfried*, make an exchange by slavishly lying between her legs attired in a shepherd's smock and performing virtuosi cunnilingus, if that is her desire.

The point is to air your wants in the sexual exchange mart, with each partner fulfilling his and her bargain. Unlike a shared bank account, neither of you can make a withdrawal without the other knowing immediately.

Memory aids

Photography

SOUVENIRS OF a truly memorable evening of love are now easily made with Polaroid cameras. Cheap and easy to use, they even have accessories that enable you to take pictures of you both at the same time. You set the machine up, move in front of it, and the picture pops out. Couples find that a simple snap elicits delightful memories and sets off the re-enactment of past glories. The Polaroid is a sex aid.

Tapes

Just as moments of rapture can be visually captured for ever, a tape recorder can store your words and sounds to be played back. Sweet words and endearing phrases are much a part of sex fun, excellent fuel for keeping the sexual home fires burning. Some couples switch their tapes on to replay a wonderful past episode, make love listening to the words they said to each other before, and reach the climax of their lovemaking in synchrony with what they did before.

Video

Videos of lovemaking combine the appeal of polaroid and tapes, and give great opportunity for endearing comments about your partner's looks, performance and affection as you watch the play back. One couple said they hadn't realised before how beautiful they actually looked together, and so a visual dimension was added to their sex lives. Expensive, perhaps, but well worth considering. As the years go by, the wonder of it grows and the bonds deepen.